Practical Messages for Spiritual Problems

by

Mrs. Oliver B. Greene

The Gospel Hour, Inc., Oliver B. Greene, Director
P. O. Box 2024, Greenville, South Carolina

Printed in the United States of America

First printing, December 1965—10,000 copies
Second printing, October 1968—15,000 copies

$4.00

FOREWORD

The writings contained in this book were first published in The Gospel Hour News, and in answer to requests from the readers they were then put into pamphlet form.

In my years as a minister's wife I have been faced with the problem of helping others solve *their* problems of a spiritual nature, and the chapters in this book were written as a means to that end.

In these brief, straightforward messages I have not attempted to display great literary talent or flawless rhetoric. I have simply tried, as honestly as I know how, to offer scriptural solutions to a few of the problems encountered by Christians, and to present God's simple plan of salvation for sinners.

As this volume goes into distribution my sincere prayer is that Christians who read it will find new inspiration and encouragement, and that those who do not *know* our wonderful Lord will find their way to salvation and eternal life in Him.

—The Author

CONTENTS

THE TWO WAYS

THE TWO WAYS

"Enter ye in at the strait gate: for wide is the gate, and broad is the way, that leadeth to destruction, and many there be which go in thereat: Because strait is the gate, and narrow is the way, which leadeth unto life, and few there be that find it" (Matt. 7:13,14).

There are two roads that lead to eternity, but they go in opposite directions. One leads to LIFE and eternity in heaven . . . the other to DEATH and eternity in hell-fire. This very moment YOU are on one of these roads! There are no sidetracks or bypasses, so do not think for one minute that you are traveling in *between* the two ways. Do not deceive yourself into thinking that you are not headed for hell, even though you *know* you are not on the road to heaven.

To the question, "Are you born again?" I frequently get this answer: "Well, I would not say I have been born again – but I am not so bad, and I do not think I will go to hell." Consider, however, what our Lord Jesus Christ said: "Ye MUST be born again" (John 3:7).

When you come to the realization that you are on one of these two roads . . . that you are not standing still, that you are not sidetracked until a more convenient time, that you are not traveling a road in between . . . then you will have reached a very important point in your life. Regardless of how nice, how clean, how moral, honest, pretty, or popular you are, *you are on the road to hell if you have not been born again.* Every step you take, every breath you breathe, every time your heart beats, you progress a little further down that road to hell.

Let us look first at the NARROW WAY.

The *only way* to get on the narrow road to heaven is *through the STRAIT GATE. That Gate is Jesus Christ.* "For there is one God, and *one mediator* between God and men, the Man Christ Jesus" (I Tim. 2:5). "I am the door: by me if any man enter in, he shall be saved . . ." (John 10:9). "In whom we have redemption through His blood, the forgiveness of sins, according to the riches of His grace" (Eph. 1:7).

The WORLD does not like this strait Gate. There are many people who have longed to be saved (or at least escape hell), but they see no night clubs, no worldly pleasures along the way. From outside the Gate, the way looks very dull and uninteresting. This Gate leads into a way that is against all natural inclinations, human passions, and lusts of the flesh.

As a whole, when the world thinks of Jesus Christ, it thinks of Him only as being another good man. Man's pride is deflated when he has to admit that he needs a Saviour. The modern teaching of the world is that everyone possesses a spark of divinity. It would be humiliating to stoop to enter the strait Gate. In their worldly-wise way, thousands of people attempt to climb around the Gate by joining the church, and thus fool themselves into thinking they are finally on the narrow way to heaven. But if they would only look around, it would be very evident to them that they are still on the road to hell.

There is one fact they have overlooked: The Bible says that *the NARROW way leads to LIFE . . .* a new life in Christ here on earth, with the ultimate goal *heaven*! It is not a road that leads just to heaven, but it leads to *real life* here on earth, as well. One does not begin to live until he has entered the Gate and received the new birth. God's Word says, "She that liveth in pleasure is dead while she liveth." It would take only a little examination on the part of the worldly-wise crowd to realize that they do not have eternal life abiding in them. "Therefore if any man be in Christ, he is a new creature: old things are passed away; behold, all things are become new" (II Cor. 5:17).

Because repentance, faith in Christ, and holiness of life have never been fashionable, the world shuns the strait Gate and the narrow way.

RELIGION does not like the strait Gate. There are religionists who heartily agree on the narrow *road* but dislike the idea of the *strait Gate*, because it is not mentioned in their book of rules and doctrines. Some religionists scoff at the idea of "just receiving Christ" as a means of salvation. That is too *easy*. Some of these devout people, therefore, have mapped out a path of self-denial, queer actions, prayers, devotions, baptisms, and persecutions. Theirs is a very narrow way indeed. They abstain from meats, wearing of jewelry, doing this and that in the name of religion . . . but *it is all in vain*, for they did not enter *the Gate*. Their narrow path is man-made, and in reality they are still on the road to hell. "Many will say to me in that day, Lord, Lord, have we not prophesied in thy name? and in thy name have cast out devils? and in thy name done many wonderful works? And then will I profess unto them, *I never knew you . . .*" (Matt. 7:22,23).

Religious but damned! They despised entering the Gate because it required too much humility. They wanted to do something to *earn* their salvation. They wanted to get to heaven by their works. But Jesus said, "*Enter ye in at the strait Gate.*" You must enter through the precious Lamb of God; there is *no other way*, no other *entrance.*

We are not SAVED by WALKING THE NARROW WAY. It is not *how* we walk or even the *walking* on the narrow road, but rather *entering the GATE* that saves us. Jesus said in John 10:9: "*I am the door*: by ME if any man enter in, he shall be saved." Again He says, ". . . And him that cometh to *me* I will in no wise cast out" (John 6:37). Also, "He that believeth on the Son (*me*) hath everlasting life" (John 3:36).

You must be born again *before* you can walk on the one road to heaven. Many people cannot see this. They look at the long, long way to heaven and then try to decide if they can really live for God. Their eyes are on the *walk of the believer* instead of on the *new birth.* They fail to consider the *Gate*—our Saviour and Lord. They never see that HE is our means to salvation . . . that He is a free Gift of God. They decide to try to merit salvation by being a "good walker" on the road of life. But they ultimately say, "I am afraid I cannot hold out – so there is no use to try." Right there they balk at the Gate!

We are not saved by QUITTING SINFUL HABITS. "But as many as *received Him*, to them gave He power to become the sons of God, even to them that believe on His name: Which were born . . . of God" (John 1:12,13). Many will argue with the very Word of God and say, "It cannot be that easy. To get in that Gate of salvation, I have to pray more and be willing to quit all my sinful habits. No, I cannot believe one is saved by just accepting Christ or just by entering in the Gate. I still believe I must live a good life to be saved."

Walking a Christ-like life is *all in the power of Christ,* and traveling the narrow road is merely evidence that we *did enter through the Gate.* Jesus said, "I am the Way"; without Him we could not walk straight. In other words, we must be born again *before* we can walk straight.

There are some precious people who greatly desire to be saved, but they are blinded by Satan. They stand trembling at the Gate wanting to enter—but look down at a cigarette between their fingers. Then they look back to the Gate, finally shake their head and say, "If I am saved, I will have to give up my cigarettes; I cannot do that." *Giving up cigarettes will not save you* – nor will smoking them damn you and send you to hell. The Bible says that salvation is found *only* in CHRIST. (The cigarettes will not directly send you to hell, but they are a pretty small excuse to use and allow the devil to keep you on the broad road to hellfire.)

Giving up cigarettes will not *help* to save you. God does not need your self-righteous acts to help Him save you! He is able to save to the uttermost all that come to Him. Stop trying to help God save you, and just let Him do a thorough job of it right now.

You are going to hell because you will not *enter the GATE* . . . you will not accept Christ as your Saviour. "He that believeth on Him is not condemned: but *he that BELIEVETH NOT is CONDEMNED ALREADY*, because he hath not believed in the name of the only begotten Son of God" (John 3:18).

"For by grace are ye saved through faith; and that *not of yourselves*: IT IS THE GIFT OF GOD: not of *works*, lest any man should boast" (Eph. 2:8,9). Even God's Word does not convince many. The pleasures of this world have a strong magnetic power. People's hearts are hardened and their eyes are blinded to the *free Gift of God*. Again and again they say, "I can't . . . I can't give up my sinful pleasures!" But I know a wonderful truth:—After a person becomes God's child, after he is born again, God gives strength and grace to overcome; He enables that person to live a clean, victorious life.

There are others who do not know what they will do about their love for movies if they go through the Gate and start out on the narrow way to heaven. My friend, do not distress yourself any longer about that; do not hesitate a minute longer to accept Christ. Do you not realize that Christ is bigger than the movies? When you enter through Jesus, you become a child of God. "Therefore if any man be in Christ, he is a new creature: old things are passed away; behold, all things are become new" (II Cor. 5:17). This does not mean that you will never be tempted with the old things again. You are still in the flesh – but inside, you are a *new man* because now Christ dwells within you. Your desires, therefore, will all be entirely different; you will now receive pleasure from things you once hated. Your whole walk of life will be changed.

The sinner does not understand how this can be true. He does not understand why a Christian does not have a desire for the things of the world, nor does he see how he can ever lose *his* desire for worldly pleasures. I Corinthians 2:14 says, "But the natural man receiveth not the things of the Spirit of God: for they are foolishness unto him: neither can he know them, because they are spiritually discerned." But if by faith you will enter the Gate, you will find no time for worldly temptations. Even if you found the *time* to participate in things of the world, you would find no real *pleasure* in them, because God's Word says, "Love not the world, neither the things that are in the world. *If any man love the world, the love of the Father is not in him*" (I John 2:15). If the love of God abides in you, you cannot love the world.

"FRIENDS" often prevent entry at the Gate. There

are some who stand at the Gate halting, wanting to enter – but they are pulled by the hands of "friends" on the one side and by the quiet wooing of the Holy Spirit on the other. As they come face to face with the decision of entering the Gate, they realize they cannot pull their friends through. The Gate is too strait and does not suit the broad views and ways of the "friends." It is a hard decision, for some of the closest friends make fun of and ridicule the narrowness of the way and the strait Gate. If the person decides to enter through the Gate, he will be ostracized by most of his worldly "friends." Some will respect his honesty and courage, however, and will honor him for the stand he takes. Some one may even possibly follow him through that Gate.

But there is a blessed truth that all who have been walking on the narrow way know: the *truest and best friend* in all the world walks with those who are on that road. His name is *Jesus*. "Having loved His own . . . He loved them to the end." He is a Friend who never ceases to love. And what is more, Jesus sees to it that the Christian, on his narrow walk, meets really good, sincere, *true* friends along the way.

We are not saved by FEELINGS. "I am the door: by me if any man enter in, he shall be saved . . ." (John 10:9). Another group seeking to walk the narrow way to heaven come face to face with the Gate and meet head-on with this verse of Scripture. But they have decided they must have some unusual vision or feeling before they can be saved. So they camp outside the Gate and pray for hours, days, sometimes weeks. Eventually one of them says: "I believe something just 'hit me,' so I must be ready now to walk the narrow way." Such people climb up on this flimsy profession and start out on *their* road to heaven without ever entering the Gate. They have only experienced an emotional feeling and have decided to "walk straight." They will readily agree that they can be saved only by receiving Christ as Saviour. But (they always put in that *but*) . . . BUT . . . they know something will "hit them" or they will have a "feeling" that will flow all through them like an electric current. They look for everything except Jesus Christ! One of the campers has climbed up high, very high – on shouting ground – because something "hit him just right"; but this emotion will soon wear off and he will doubt his experience – and soon be worse off than before. He must have a true *heart* experience.

Sad but true, there are earnest souls still camping outside the Gate, waiting for God to send that "feeling." There are sincere people who have waited outside for years, because they do not know or else will not believe that *when we ENTER THROUGH THE DOOR we are saved.*

We enter that door by *faith.* God will never give a person camping on the outside a special feeling to prove he is saved–because *there IS NO SALVATION outside the Lord Jesus Christ.* God's Word says that as many as *receive Him* shall be saved (John 1:12) and that "whosoever shall call upon the name of the Lord shall be saved" (Rom. 10:13). God said it! Why lower God to man's way by demanding proof that He will keep His Word? We enter the door by *faith*, by *believing His Word.* "Him that cometh to me, I will in no wise cast out." Stop doubting God, and by faith enter in TODAY!

"Being born again . . . by the Word of God, which liveth and abideth for ever" (I Pet. 1:23). Do not treat the Word of God lightly or doubt it, for Jesus said, "He that rejecteth me, and receiveth not MY WORDS, hath one that judgeth him: the WORD that I have spoken, the same shall judge him in the last day" (John 12:48). The Word of God will *save* you NOW – but if you reject it, it will *judge* you in the last day.

The Scripture does not say in vain, "For the preaching of the Cross is to them that perish foolishness; but unto us which are saved it is the power of God" (I Cor. 1:18). We who have entered the Gate and walk the narrow way find its narrowness is not confining, but rather that it gives freedom and great liberty. "Ye shall know the truth, and the truth shall make you free" (John 8:32).

There are no glittering, brilliantly-lighted playhouses of sinful pleasures on the narrow road to heaven; but life is filled with righteousness, peace, joy, faith, hope, contentment, and love. We who are on this narrow way do not find it dull and uninteresting. Time does not lag on our hands; on the contrary, there is so much to do we cannot find time to do it all. One of the remarkable things about those who have entered through the Gate and are traveling the narrow way is that *NOT ONE is sorry he chose this way.* That is something which cannot be said about the travelers on the devil's superhighway. True peace and satisfaction are not given by the devil . . . they are found only in and through the Lord Jesus Christ. *He alone* can satisfy the soul.

Those who have entered *the Gate* do not find the way difficult. Sometimes there are hills to climb and valleys to cross, but they can all be crossed by faith. "This is the victory that overcometh the world, even our faith" (I John 5:4). Christ has promised to go with us all the way . . . even in the darkest valleys. We are not alone! And although we travel the way of the *Cross*, we know that at the end is our eternal home in heaven with *crowns* for the faithful. The narrow road is the road to victory, and *Christ*—the victorious One—is the BEGINNING, the END, and the WAY between. Thank God, I have entered the strait Gate . . . *have you*?

Let us look briefly now at the BROAD WAY.

This gate is very wide and easily entered because it does not oppose, in any way, the lusts of the flesh or any selfish desires. It does not hinder natural inclinations. There are no barriers or obstructions. Not one selfish deed or sinful pleasure has to be sacrificed. Every inch is well lighted with neon signs offering pleasures, sins, supposed "good times," and laughter. Satan stands at the entrance as an *angel of light* to lure the unsuspecting sinner through the door, which appears enticing and alluring. He stands there to convince the would-be sojourner that the place called *hell* could not be connected in any way with this beautiful beginning. The *angel of light* convinces many that only "nit-wits" choose the *narrow* Gate. Pleasure, happiness, good times, youth, and the philosophy of "I have only one life to live" beckon with many hands. It all seems so harmless and reasonable that the vast majority of the crowd pass through this gate and rush pell-mell down this superhighway.

Many choose the broad way simply because the majority are going that way. They decide to "follow the crowd," for they are afraid to be found with the minority. They are allergic to criticism and are afraid to stand alone. In spineless subjection they follow the mob headed for hell!

There is room on this broad way for all types of people. In fact, the way is so broad that the devil can keep the morally good person, the religious-but-lost person, the thief, the liar, the drunkard, and all the rest traveling without a jostle.

The self-righteous church member congratulates himself that he is not in the gutter like the drunkard; yet he is on the same highway, traveling the same direction. The morally clean woman holds her skirts tightly about her to keep from ever touching a degraded harlot; yet she is on the same road, traveling to the same destination. The devil does not care how good a person is, or in what condition he is when he reaches hell – just so he *goes* there. The only thing that concerns the devil is that the person does not receive Christ as his Saviour while he has the opportunity.

When a person first enters the broad way, it does not appear to be evil. The devil is smart. He sees to it that a person begins with *little* things. Should the conscience prick just a little, Satan quiets it by saying, "This little thing is not wrong," or "Just this little pleasure will not hurt you any."

A six-year-old child begins school in the *first grade*– not in *college*. Year by year he advances until finally the last year of college is reached. Just so, the devil starts the sinner in the "first grade" of "innocent" sins and pleasures. But step by step, mile by mile, down the road he reaches a maturity of sin.

There are many reading this message who have been warned many times about certain sins and the folly of putting off salvation. But there is always the thought, "I can take care of myself." There was not the realization of Satan's power, though – and now you, dear reader, find that you were not master of your own soul. You are far down the road and deep in trouble.

Yes, the broad way looks smooth and easy at first . . . but there are thousands today who can tell you that there are untold pitfalls, troubles, and heartaches. God's Word says, "The way of transgressors is hard" (Prov. 13:15) and that "the wages of sin is death" (Rom. 6:23).

Even though many discover that the things on this road have brought them no peace or satisfaction, they continue on down the road–ever searching for that which will satisfy. Some are snatched off the road at an early age and cast into hell-fire. But there are multitudes who spend many years traveling this way only to find themselves at the end with no peace, no happiness, no precious promises. They find nothing but the wide open mouth of hell waiting to swallow them up. Facing them is not only the memory of a wasted and doomed life, but even more terrible – an eternity to remember and be tortured in hell.

Yes, *there are TWO WAYS.* And there are two greatly contrasted gates. The *strait Gate* represents the death of the precious Lamb of God . . . and to those who enter it, it means *death to self.* The Apostle Paul wrote, "I am crucified with Christ. . . ." Again he wrote, "Likewise reckon ye yourselves to be dead indeed to sin . . . ." Although it begins with death, *the strait Gate ends with eternal life.*

The *wide gate* at the beginning represents life, but it ends with *eternal death.* Dear reader, when you reached the age of accountability, if you rejected Christ as your Saviour, you stepped through the wide gate and on to the broad way. But you do not have to continue traveling on it. Will you not this very moment change highways? Accept Christ and enter through the narrow Gate. Would you not like to start walking on the narrow road to eternal life?

Do not forget–if you are not born again, you are *lost.* If you are not on the narrow way to heaven, then you are on the broad way to hell. I pray for you to accept Christ *now* and *begin to really live.*

DEATH IN DELAY

DEATH IN DELAY

"Boast not thyself of to morrow; for thou knowest not what a day may bring forth" (Prov. 27:1).

The business of our soul's salvation should definitely be the most important thing on earth to us, since it is through salvation alone that we may have an eternal home in heaven; but though this matter of salvation is urgent, it is seldom considered so, and is put off day after day as if times and seasons are at our whimsical disposal. The Bible solemnly declares, "Except a man be born again, he cannot see the kingdom of God" (John 3:3b). Again, "Except ye repent, ye shall all likewise perish" (Luke 13:3,5).

Not only does the *Bible* warn that salvation is important (IMPERATIVE) if we are to spend eternity in heaven, but God also speaks to you *in your own heart*, convicting you of sin and calling you to repentance. How many times have you—even you who do not read the Bible—been reminded that everything in your life is wrong, and that it is high time you started thinking of your eternal welfare? Do you not at times admit to yourself that you are weary in your soul from fighting God; weary of carrying the burden of guilt which weights you down? Are you not weary of the emptiness of the world which you serve? What will you reply to that inner voice that has for so long spoken to your heart? What excuse do you offer?

There are numerous excuses sinners use for not accepting Christ, but in this message I want to discuss those most frequently used:

First — *the excuses in which GOD IS ACCUSED.*

Second—*the one in which the SINNER HIMSELF IS EXCUSED.*

Accusing God

I.

When many people are approached about their soul's salvation, they will say that *God has not yet given them the necessary help and strength to live for Him*, and that in their present condition they would "never make it"; so, in this underhanded way, they accuse God of being the reason they are not saved. They continue to delay their conversion by flattering themselves that one day they will be less attached to this world. They comfort their heart with the falsehood that sometime in the future, when God really GETS READY to save them, He will remove all obstacles, knock them down, and *make* them be saved!

This business of blaming God began with the very first man. Adam said, "Lord, the woman you gave me caused me to sin." In other words, he said, "God, *you* are really to blame, because had you not given me the woman, I would not have sinned." Such is the reasoning of almost all souls living in guilt, who delay conversion until a future day . . . a conversion which is so important that God says, "What shall it profit a man, if he shall gain the whole world, and *lose his own soul*?"

The blackest of sinners can often argue the loudest and longest on religious subjects. They can finish almost any verse of Scripture the personal worker starts to quote—but with all of their head-knowledge, the heart is "desperately wicked." Like a parrot, they continually repeat (as sinners often do) that conversion does not depend upon *them*; that instead it is the Lord who must change the heart and give to them the faith and grace which they, as yet, do not have. Thus, they are not satisfied with provoking God's wrath by trampling the Son of God under foot (Heb. 10:29), but they further insult Him by laying on Him the blame for their sinful state. Some of them have said that if they had faith (which God alone can give) they would be saved. But when they speak of "saving faith," what do they mean? No doubt, some actually mean "faith in the Bible, faith in God, faith in eternity."

Somewhere down the line, they have allowed doubts to creep in and they have put a question mark around God's Word – but of all the peoples of the world, *Americans* have no right to offer such an excuse. Our nation was founded on the principles of Christianity; our Constitution and system of government were based on the Word of God. Even our money has inscribed upon it, "In God we trust." On nearly every street corner here in America, there is a church testifying to the reality of a God and of a Saviour– and from earliest childhood we have been reminded of a holy God. "The heavens declare the glory of God; and the firmament sheweth His handywork" (Psa. 19:1).

You have not *always* had doubts about God's Word, so what have you done with the faith you once had? People become doubters and skeptics for various and sundry reasons. For example:

Doubts have come to some as the result of a dead orthodoxy. They have long associated with people who have a dead religion; consequently, they judge all professing Christians by these people, and eventually doubt the Bible, which speaks of a real, living Christ.

Doubts are easily acquired by being too broad-minded and studying all kinds of cults and religions, supplanting truth with confusion.

Doubts may arise from being disappointed by a friend, or from an unfortunate church affair.

Doubts too often arise from a little learning acquired in atheistic schools where the Bible is denied and the miracles of the Bible are set forth as "myths" or "fables."

In this day of modern skepticism, whatever your reason for doubting, you had better stop making excuses, and cling to the faith of our fathers.

One man said, "The lesson of life is to believe what the years and the centuries say against the hours." You KNOW the Bible has stood the test of time, and your doubting will not change it. Even *you* (if you are a true doubter) sometimes doubt your own doubts. The ONLY SAFE AND SURE PLACE to stand is *on the Word of God.*

I ask you again, "What have you done with the faith you once had? Is it not that you have dragged this precious gift through the corruption of a sinful life until you have become hardened and your conscience seared? Could it not be that a moral aversion to the truth causes you to doubt? Are you truly an 'honest doubter'?" I sincerely believe that many men doubt The Book that condemns them, and use their doubts as an excuse to cover their low-pitched life. Are you one who, in the satisfying of your lustful passions, has extinguished the light you inherited in the faith of your fathers?

2.

A second group of people—who do not go so far as to say they *doubt* the Word—*put a different meaning upon the faith* they accuse God of *not* giving them. They say, "I have tried to be saved, but I do not have enough faith." They think of "saving faith" as some sort of emotional, hair-raising experience that happens when God forces that faith upon them. Whether or not they are honest in their belief, I do not know. At least, that is their excuse—an excuse which is contrary to the Word of God. Our Heavenly Father did not force Adam into *His* choice, but gave to Adam the moral right to choose for himself. God does not FORCE saving faith upon us.

Assuming some of you are honest in your belief that you do not have enough faith to be saved, I will endeavor to show you *what faith is* and *how it is acquired*:

"Faith is the substance of things hoped for, the evidence of things not seen" (Heb. 11:1).

"Faith cometh by hearing, and hearing by the Word of God" (Rom. 10:17).

God's Word is the instrument God has appointed (and which He uses) to impart saving faith. We are not to look for faith as some mysterious ingredient that comes in small, medium, or large packages. It is not to be expected to cause internal or external chills, thrills, goose-pimples, or an upset nervous system! *Faith is simply BELIEVING GOD.* Those who sincerely doubt the Word of God and yet have a desire to know the truth, should read the Word. Go to the Bible with an open mind. The condition of all conditions lies in the ATTITUDE with which the truth-seeker approaches the Bible in his search for truth. *Faith comes through the Word.* Galatians 5:22 says, "But the fruit of the Spirit is love, joy, peace, longsuffering, gentleness, goodness, FAITH." The Word is the instrument by which faith comes, but the Holy Spirit carries the Word home to the heart. Therefore, sinner, you will be aided by God's Holy Spirit in your search for truth; you do not have to do it all alone (I John 2:27).

How much faith do you need to search for the truth? Only "faith as a grain of mustard seed" . . . only enough faith in things eternal to cause you to DESIRE to know the truth, to desire to be saved. But no amount of praying, begging, or searching will bring faith if we neglect God's instrument, His Word.

If you want "saving faith," then use the faith you have. Read the Word, and God's Holy Spirit will help you to believe the Word. You who complain that God has not given you faith, have the wrong conception of faith. You think in terms of faith that "removes mountains," and you will accept no explanation of any other kind. In your foolish heart you say, "All—or nothing!" And because you have not yet acquired the faith to move mountains and raise the dead, you travel on in unbelief, on your way to hell.

In Mark 9, a father came to Jesus seeking help for his son, who had a dumb spirit. In verse 22, the child's father said, ". . . IF thou canst do any thing, have compassion on us, and help us." Then Jesus answering said, "If thou canst believe, all things are possible to him that believeth." The father said, "Lord, I believe; HELP THOU MINE UNBELIEF." This imperfect faith satisfied Jesus, and He healed the son. Sinner—you who use the refrain, "I do not have enough faith"—use what faith you have, and through the Word your faith will be increased.

I am afraid it is not *faith* that most of you lack, but the desire to fulfill the duties faith imposes on you! It is not your DOUBTS that keep you from believing, but your *sinful life*. Therefore, faith appears difficult to you—not because it is hard to acquire, but because, when applied, it regulates the life and the actions. You realize that a man who has been saved "by grace through faith" will not act as you do – and you are just not willing and ready to come out of the cesspools of the devil. Why not be honest and admit that it is not faith you lack, but willingness to turn your back on sin and the devil? You are heldback from seeking salvation because of the high standards of life salvation requires. To sum up the matter, it is your corrupted life that you love and hold on to, and not the fact that you cannot have faith.

3.

Some of you may complain that you are *waiting for God to bring conviction to your heart.* You delay conversion on the pretext that since salvation is of God, and God alone can change the heart, you must wait until conviction comes. However, we are told in II Peter 3:9 that "The Lord is . . . *not willing that ANY should perish*, but that ALL should come to repentance."

The simple truth is, you have no inward desire to live for God; therefore you say that God has not yet convicted you. You say that if God wanted you to serve Him, He would change your desires, and instead of a taste for worldly things He would give you a desire for only *spiritual* things. Oh, unjust man—to accuse God of not doing His part in your soul's salvation! To accuse God of not bringing conviction to your heart is unjust and deceitful.

For what are you looking when you say you are waiting for God to bring conviction? God has shown His mercies in a thousand ways. He has kept you alive through countless dangers, when you could have been hurled into a Christless eternity! Do you not feel grateful at all, that you are alive right now, with another chance to be saved, rather than begging for a drop of water in hell-fire?

By His mercies He has called you over and over again. Through circumstances, through sorrows and troubles, He has called you—and through this process, He has kept your heart softened and prevented you from finding tranquillity in guilt. A just and merciful God has urged you and pursued you everywhere. You who complain that you have not been called or convicted are either deceiving yourselves, or the devil has sadly deceived you as to what "conviction" is.

To some, this no doubt seems an exaggerated account of sinners, and they cannot understand why I even take up time and space to discuss it. I assure you there are a great many sinners who are even worse than I have pictured, because I do not have the words nor the ability to portray their darkened fancies when it comes to salvation. I have seen women actually shaking under conviction, and when I asked them to call upon God for salvation, they would say, "I am not under enough conviction. When God really convicts, I will not be able to stand back, but will be forced to be saved. God is not ready to save me yet." By their excuse, I gather that they are waiting for a movement from God that will completely lift them out of themselves without any willing move on their own part, and they will be motivated by an outside power that will force them to fall on their knees, asking God to save them. How wrong! How deceived these people are! GOD WILL NOT SAVE YOU AGAINST YOUR WILL. If you are convicted that you are a sinner, that you are on your road to hell, and that Jesus loves you and wants to save you, that is conviction enough. Conviction means to "convince someone" . . . and *convince* means "to bring by argument to belief beyond doubt."

The Bible says in John 16:8: "And when He (speaking of the Holy Spirit) is come, He will reprove (or CONVINCE) the world of sin, and of righteousness, and of judgment." Therefore, all the conviction you need from the Holy Spirit is to be convinced that you are a sinner, convinced that Jesus will save you, and convinced that there is only one step between you and death! If you are truly convinced of this, you will not hesitate to do something about it. It is not that God has not brought deep enough conviction – but I am afraid you will not allow yourself to be truly convinced that you are actually on the road to hell, without hope, and that you may drop at any moment into the fire that is never quenched. You close your ears to the truth and harden your heart to God's call.

4.

Some people complain that *God has not done anything for them.* They have the idea that all they have to do is wait for God to change them with a lightning-like stroke, changing them so completely inside and out that they will then be ready to live for Christ. And this they expect without any effort on their part. They say, "When I am saved, I want to be saved all the way"–which is all right if they mean it. But they do not. They think that, in their present state, salvation would involve too many sacrifices and that it is up to God to give grace so that when they believe, they will be converted without any sacrifice on their part . . . without any self-denial, and almost without being aware of it themselves.

These people are like the man who said that if God wanted him to stop smoking, He would remove the taste of tobacco from his mouth. Some sinners claim that when God wants to save them, He will remove all passions, all temptations, and all desire for sinful pleasures. They want no other kind of salvation–and before they will even consider salvation, they want the assurance that God has done all this for them. They say they do not intend to be a hypocrite – but to sit around waiting for salvation on this basis is to act the fool.

God sent Jesus Christ as Saviour into the world. He

gave us an open Bible, which tells us of a heaven to gain and a hell to shun. The Bible tells us that we are born in sin and "shapen in iniquity" and that "we are by nature the children of wrath." It tells us that before we can go to heaven, we must be born again – and to be born again is to accept Jesus Christ as Saviour. The Bible is very clear in showing us that we do not have to go to hell – that we can go to heaven if we so desire; the choice is up to us. "Choose you this day whom ye will serve" (Josh. 24:15).

"As many as received Him, to them gave He power to become the sons of God . . ." (John 1:12). Of those who would *not* receive Him, Jesus said, "And ye will not come to me, that ye might have life" (John 5:40).

The Bible tells us that we are born again by the Word (I Peter 1:23) and "By grace are ye saved through faith" (Eph. 2:8). God's grace is ours when we receive Jesus Christ through faith in His Word – but when we are born again, we need not expect to immediately become sinless saints or full-grown Christians.

There is not a particle of use in sinners blaming God for their not being saved. They are sailing under false colors, deceiving themselves. All they need to do is stop blaming God, and come to Him as any other humble sinner, asking Him to save them.

Ignorance is no excuse. The Bible gives the plan of salvation and also teaches us, "As newborn babes, desire the sincere milk of the Word, that ye may grow thereby" (I Pet. 2:2). There is no place in the Bible where God implies that we are to sit around and wait for Him to completely overpower us, save us whether we are willing or not . . . and make us into such a saint that from then on the angels in heaven will have no more spotless, perfect lives than we.

Sinner, if you are guilty of such a foolish attitude, be honest with yourself and stop blaming God because you are still a sinner. It is not that God WILL NOT give you faith; it is not that He will not convict you; it is not that He will not give you grace to overcome all passions and temptations – but it is rather that YOU WILL NOT BE SAVED. The answer is YOU! If God forced grace upon you, you would be sorry that it came and broke the chains of worldliness, which you still love. If you are not saved, rest assured it is not God's fault. It is *your* fault, and yours alone.

Sinners Excuse Themselves

Sinners comfort themselves, saying it is impossible just now for them to live for God. They declare that at some future date they will be less attached to the world. Many sinners want to put off salvation until they are older. They say they want the years of youth to pass away, and then they will not mind living a life dedicated to the Lord. They really think it is unfair for anyone to expect them to live a pious life while they are young and having a good time. They intend to settle down "one of these days," and then they will do business with God – and thus they excuse themselves.

I ask these people, "Who has told you that your mind will ever change? Who guarantees that the time will ever come when you are READY to settle down?" The question above all questions is: "Who guarantees that you will live to a ripe old age?" But, even granting that YOU MAY have a long life and may live out your allotted threescore and ten years, will old age change your mind about sin? Did old age prepare Solomon to live a better life? No, it was in older life that his passions rose the highest and his shameful living knew no bounds. Years of living in sin will only serve to harden your conscience, and it will be harder to accept Christ in older life than it is now.

Do you realize what you propose to do? You propose to live the best years of your life for the devil, and give the dregs to the Lord. It is precisely as if you said to God, "Lord, so long as I shall be fit for the world and its pleasures, think not that I shall seek Thee or turn toward Thee. So long as the world shall be pleased with me, I can never think of devoting myself to Thee. Later, when I am too old to have any pleasures in the world, I will turn to Thee for salvation . . . (for I feel that salvation is for old people and little children)."

I fear you plan to burn the candle of life for the devil, and then blow the smoke in God's face. Your excuse that if you now give your heart to God you are afraid you "could not hold out," is equivalent to saying that you do not trust God to keep His Word, keeping you and giving you grace to live for Him.

You depend upon His mercies while insulting Him—but you dare not trust Him to sustain you while LIVING for Him! You have shut your eyes and deceived yourself into thinking that you have nothing to risk in putting off salvation, and that a merciful God will not damn you without a chance. Yet you do not have this same confidence when it comes to your *serving* Him.

Thou art inexcusable, O man. So, I beg you to come to Jesus today, "making your calling and election sure." As a sinner you stand before God condemned: "He that believeth on Him is not condemned: but *he that believeth not is CONDEMNED ALREADY*, because *he hath not believed* in the name of the only begotten Son of God" (John 3:18).

God is not to blame for your lost condition; neither

are you excused – therefore, in the name of Jesus, I ask you to stop giving excuses and let this be the last moment you put off your salvation. Be saved NOW! "Behold, *now* is the accepted time; behold, *now* is the day of salvation" (II Cor. 6:2).

THE CONDEMNATION OF SIN

THE CONDEMNATION OF SIN

"Her sins, which are many, are forgiven; for she loved much: but to whom little is forgiven, the same loveth little" (Luke 7:47).

A lady once said to me, "I wish I had been a very wicked, wayward, immoral woman before I was saved, so that there would have been a greater change in my life after accepting Christ." She went on to say that she could have loved her Saviour more had she been a drunkard, a harlot, or a thief. I disagreed with her then – and I disagree with her now. A woman does not have to be changed from a harlot to a lady to love Christ MUCH . . . she only has to have the right conception of sin.

The person who feels that he (or she) has been forgiven *little* may well have doubts as to whether he has been forgiven *at all.* Those who have such high regard for their own righteousness and inward good, will love Christ but little. An outstanding minister in a large church would not allow his church to sing "Amazing grace, how sweet the sound, that saved a wretch like me." He said he did not want to sing a lie, and he could not sing "that saved a wretch like me" because he had never *been* a wretch! (Such a man is *still* a wretch and does not know it.)

Too many prove by their scanty, formal services that they have no proper sense of their guilt, nor do they have the right perspective of the sacrifice of the Lamb of God, who made their forgiveness possible. If you feel that you were forgiven "little," you should seek for a clearer view of your own vileness and of the Christian's obligation to Christ.

I do not mean to imply that to be a vile sinner one has to reach the depths of sin as *man* labels sin. There are serious results of such sins: A bitter harvest is reaped in body and mind because of these sins, even after a person is saved – and should such a one never receive Christ, the degree of suffering in hell would be greater for his exceeding sinfulness. But it requires the *same* grace to save the *moral* sinner as to save the one who has sinned outrageously. NO SINNER WHO HAS BEEN SAVED BY THE GRACE OF GOD WAS FORGIVEN LITTLE!

We are ALL "born in sin and shapen in iniquity," and without Christ we are undone, dead in trespasses and sins, and doomed to an eternal hell. *Sin is a debt* – and whether we consider the debt small or large, it is *still* too great for us to pay.

"ALL we like sheep have gone astray; we have turned *every one* to his own way; and the Lord hath laid on *Him* the iniquity of us ALL" (Isa. 53:6). It takes the blood of Jesus Christ to cleanse us from sin–whether we be moral or immoral, good or bad. I repeat: *Any sinner saved by grace has been forgiven MUCH.* Paul the Apostle was not a drunken gutter rat. He was very religious and upright . . . a clean-living, devout Pharisee; but after he was converted he said he was "chief of sinners."

I want us to study the parable of the two debtors in Luke 7:36–50, as spoken by Jesus to Simon the Pharisee. Simon invited Jesus to his house for a meal. While He was there, a woman who was a great sinner (in the sense of unchastity) came, bringing an alabaster box of ointment to anoint the Saviour's feet. She washed His feet with her tears, dried them with her hair, and anointed them with the expensive ointment. Simon was disgusted, not liking this performance of worship at all. He said, "If this man

(Jesus) were a prophet, He would know what manner of woman this is that toucheth Him." Simon was self-righteous, not realizing his own need for cleansing. Therefore, Jesus gave him this parable.

There were two debtors who had all things common (except for one thing):

Both were debtors,

Both had nothing,

Both could pay nothing,

Both were under obligation to the creditor,

Both were ready for debtor's prison.

The only difference in their situations was in the amount of their respective debts. Yet the one who owed *fifty* pence could no more pay *his* debt than could the one who owed *five hundred* pence. It would not have made any difference had they owed *ten thousand* pence . . . they could have paid it as easily at that moment as they could have paid the fifty and the five hundred pence–for the sum total of their capital was NOTHING. The debts of *both* were too heavy to bear–and if they had owed only *one fifth* of their respective debts it still would not have lessened the burden, because they had *nothing* with which to pay.

The creditor forgave them both. Jesus asked of Simon, "Which of them will love him most?" Simon said, "I suppose (I imagine, I presume) . . . the one who was forgiven most." (The Bible dictionary says, "The original word *suppose* has a shade of supercilious irony as though Simon thought the question very trivial, and never dreamed that it could have any bearing upon himself.") Jesus said, "Thou hast rightly judged, Simon . . . the one will love MUCH who realizes that he has been *forgiven* much."

The purpose of this parable was to rebuke Simon, who

in cold calculation considered *his* debt to be much less than the *woman's* debt. *But was it?*

One commentary says, "Cold selfishness does not take itself to be sinful. Simon imagined he had little to be forgiven, and therefore he loved little. Had he been a true saint he would have recognized his debt. The confessions of the holiest are also the most heart-rending, because they most fully recognize the true nature of sin. What is needed to waken MUCH LOVE is not MUCH SIN, for we all have that qualification; but a deep sense of sin." Any Christian will testify that the closer he gets to God and the more he grows in grace, the more he realizes the magnitude of his sin before he was saved.

Simon showed his doubt that Jesus was the Christ when he said, "IF He were a prophet . . . ." He showed his lack of love and respect when he did not even offer Jesus the usual courtesies customarily offered to any guest. Simon was truly a "wretch" and did not recognize that fact. The amount of his debt was rapidly mounting—and he did not even see it.

The *woman*, because of her open transgressions, recognized her position, and knew that she had been forgiven much. Knowing that she had been *forgiven* much, recognizing the greatness of her debt of sin, she *loved* much.

One debtor in the parable did not have as many dollar marks against his name as did the other; yet he had a debt that was too heavy for him to bear. It was enough to cast him into prison, for he could pay absolutely nothing—not even a penny—on his debt. The fifty pence he owed looked as large to him as the other debtor's *five hundred* pence looked to *him.* If he considered it a burden too heavy to bear, then there really should be no difference in the relief and thankfulness of the two men.

It would indeed have been unthankful for the debtor to say, "My master forgave me only fifty pence—and that is nothing compared to the five hundred pence he forgave my fellowman." To a man who had nothing, either debt is staggering, and the men should be equally thankful. Simon should have realized this fact—but he did not. Surely Jesus was rebuking the self-righteousness of Simon, who considered his a fifty-pence debt, and considered that he had been forgiven so little.

Dr. William R. Newell, in his book on Romans, relates this incident:

Rev. Rowland Hill, at the close of a great meeting, saw a lady riding in an elegant carriage, who commanded her coachman to halt, and beckoned Mr. Hill to approach her.

"Sir," she said, "my coachman came to your meetings and says you told him how to be saved; so that he is now very happy. Please tell me how a lady of the nobility is to be saved, for I also desire to be happy."

"Madam," said the preacher, "Christ died for the whole world. God says there is no difference. All are to be saved through simple faith in Him."

"Do you mean," she said haughtily, "that I must be saved in the same way as my coachman?"

"Precisely. There is no other way."

"Then," she said, "I will have none of it!" and she made her coachman drive away.

The essential foundation of all right appreciation of the Saviour is a right view of the sin from which He has delivered us. We should have a knowledge of the *nature* of sin, the *evil* of sin, and the *condemnation* of sin. One cannot fully understand what Christ has done to save us, without first learning what sin has done to ruin us. One cannot estimate the exceeding preciousness of redemption without first realizing the completeness and (as far as *we* are concerned) the hopelessness of our condemnation. To minimize either the preciousness of salvation or the completeness of condemnation is to fall far short of loving the Saviour MUCH.

What Is Sin?

The answer to this question is given in I John 3:4: "For *sin is the transgression of the law.*" Concerning sin in general–not against God, but against any human government–the same answer applies. Sin or crime anywhere is transgression of the law. When a law is instituted, regardless of what it concerns, the fulfillment of that law is *innocence*, and the violation of that law is *guilt.* If there be no law, there can be no transgression and consequently no sin. "For by the law is the knowledge of sin" (Rom. 3:20b).

Considering sin against God, defined as the transgression of God's Law, you see that all depends upon what the Law is. I do not think we will have any difficulty here, for the simple answer is *the revealed will of God.* We must not think that the Law here refers only to the Ten Commandments or to the Law of Moses. In its broader meaning it covers more than just the commandments given to Moses on Mt. Sinai. I looked up the word "Law" in several commentaries and found that sometimes the whole of the Old Testament is spoken of as The Law. In Hebrews 10:16 we read, "This is the covenant that I will make with them after those days, saith the Lord, *I will put my laws into their hearts, and in their minds will I write them.*"

It matters not how the revealed will of God is made

known to us—whether by voice of our own conscience, or in the written Word; whether we hear it thunder from Sinai, or our teacher be the mercies of Calvary—*however* we learn the will of God for us, *that is Law.* In a sense, all of the Gospel is Law. It tells of a Saviour and demands that we believe on Him—or perish. "*Ye must be born again*" is a definite scriptural command. The command to repent is a law of God, and if we do not repent, we transgress God's Law – and we perish.

Sin, then, is *the transgression of the Law* – and –

The Law of God Is Perfect

The laws of human government are imperfect and inadequate because they can govern only the *outward deeds* of man; but *God's* Law reaches to the *inner* man. There is no part of man that God's Law does not cover perfectly. God looks upon the heart, and therefore He makes laws for the heart. Out of the *heart* proceed the issues of life, and only *God's* Law reaches the heart. God's Law is perfect. Nothing in or about us is too minute or secret to come under its provisions.

Perfect Law Requires Perfect Obedience

God could not be a holy and just God if He made laws and then ignored or excused the *transgression* of those laws. Any *man*-made law requires complete obedience, and to say that only *part* of it demands obedience is to say that only part of it is *law.* The part you say does not require complete obedience, transgression of which may be tolerated, is not law at all. It may be advice—but it is not LAW.

Whatever is law requires complete obedience, and the transgression of it is sin. *God's Law* is His revealed will to us. It is perfect, and it requires complete obedience.

Whatever falls short of or transgresses any part of God's Law is sin – whether in outward deed, inward thought, or affection.

"What!!!???" you might ask in alarm. "Can I fail in *nothing*–not even a *thought*–and it not be sin?" You can answer that for yourself if you will repeat the definition of sin: "*Sin is the transgression of the law.*"

In James 2:10 we read, "Whosoever shall keep the whole law, and yet offend in one point, he is guilty of all." The meaning is not that to violate one command is to be guilty of all sins such as adultery, murder, and drunkenness; but the Law of God is ONE. To break it in one point is to break its oneness, thus putting the lawbreaker under condemnation. The Law is of many precepts, many links. To break one link in the whole is to break the chain as completely as if all links were broken. *One sin*, then, makes us guilty – and we have violated the *whole Law*.

Galatians 3:10 says, "Cursed is every one that continueth not in all things which are written in the book of the law to do them." In other words, "Condemned is he to the penalty of the law who continueth not *in all things* written in the book of the law." You observe the condition of the covenant continuance in ALL things–not just *part* of them for *part* of your life, but ALL of them for ALL of your life.

You say then, "Is there no hope for me? I could never obey all the laws all of the time. It is impossible!!" Yes, it *is* impossible for you to keep all of the law all of the time from the moment you are born until you die; but that is where our blessed Saviour comes in: "For what the law could not do, in that it was weak through the flesh, God sending His own Son in the likeness of sinful flesh, and for sin, condemned sin in the flesh: That the righteousness of the law might be fulfilled in us, who walk not after the flesh, but after the Spirit" (Rom. 8:3,4).

Realizing the truth of this Scripture, you surely must recognize that you are a transgressor of the Law. How often you have transgressed is not possible to know. The important thing right now is to know you ARE a transgressor. God can exact from you all the penalty of a law entirely broken. There is no use in your counting up your good points, such as honesty, good intentions, and morality—for they will avail you nothing. You have broken the Law, and nothing you can do will ever undo that. Oh, the wretched, miserable condition of a sinner, *if Jesus Christ had not died*! "Wherefore, as by one man sin entered into the world, and death by sin; and so death passed upon all men, for that all have sinned. . . But not as the offence, so also is the free gift. For if through the offence of one many be dead, much more the grace of God, and the gift by grace, which is by one man, Jesus Christ, hath abounded unto many. . . That as sin hath reigned unto death, even so might grace reign through righteousness unto eternal life by Jesus Christ our Lord" (Rom. 5:12, 15,21).

A Sinner Is Condemned Now

One of the strongest influences in keeping men from realizing the awfulness of sin and from coming to God is their idea that they are not lost NOW. They continue in their sinful state, laboring under the misapprehension that they are not lost now—but *will be lost someday* if they are not saved. They willingly accept the false theory that their eternal destiny is not to be decided until judgment day. In the meantime, they cling to the childish idea that they are sending up good works and bad works, and hope that the good deeds outweigh the bad. It seems they have a notion that God does not see sin as soon as it is committed, nor see the sinner's heart–NOW–but that He is waiting until judgment day to decide the sinner's fate. It is possible that such people compare God's judgment with trials in the courts of our land. They know that in the courts under our system of laws, there can be no condemnation until a man has had a formal trial. It is assumed that a man is innocent until proven guilty, and it is only by examination and through witnesses that the truth can be determined. After all the evidence is in, the jurors decide "guilty" or "not guilty," and the judge passes sentence.

There are those who think the judgment day is for the purpose of ascertaining guilt. They believe they will be examined, their good deeds balanced against the bad deeds –and then God the Judge will determine their future. *No! This is not so.* The day of God's judgment is not to unveil evidence to God, for He knows NOW every thought and every secret of the heart. God's judgment is not that He may form a decision as to whether a person will be lost or saved–for that is settled at the time of death. Each moment of our lives we are perfectly known and weighed in the balance of God's Law. We are either *lost NOW*–or *saved NOW*. John 3:18 tells us, "He that believeth on Him (the Son) is not condemned." Right now, he who has taken Christ as Saviour is free from condemnation. Judgment has already been passed–and *he is free*. "If the Son . . . shall make you free, ye shall be free indeed" (John 8:36). But the remaining part of John 3:18 says, "He that believeth *not* is *condemned ALREADY . . . .*" Condemned *right now* . . . not "going to be" condemned at the judgment day–but *is condemned RIGHT NOW*.

Now let us sum up what we have discussed:

A single transgression of the Law makes you liable to the penalty of the whole Law. "The wages of sin is death." Whether few sins or many sins, whether great sins or small transgressions, sin results in death . . . *spiritual* death in an eternal, burning hell. There is no use to argue, as many do, that though sinners, they have not sinned *to this extent* or *that extent*. We beg those people to hear God's Word, and recognize the fact that the *extent* to which they have sinned is not the question. "Sin is the transgression of the law" . . . whether ONE sin or a *thousand* sins . . . and condemnation follows sin.

You are not capable of determining the AMOUNT of your transgression. To say that you have not been so bad—or that, though a sinner, you are a *morally good* sinner, is to say that you are not convinced of your sins and up to now have no real conception of sin in its terrible nature. What do you imagine your life looks like in the eyes of a holy and righteous God? If you have not been saved—whether you consider yourself a big sinner or a little sinner—you stand before God CONDEMNED . . . NOW! You are under the wrath of God, and your only hope is in Christ Jesus, who died for sinners. The blood of Jesus Christ cleanses from all sin.

Good or bad, YOU cannot do away with even one little sin. God could not be just and holy if He overlooked your transgression of the Law; but He sent Jesus to take your place, to make an atonement for sin—and now He can be "just, and the justifier of him which believeth in Jesus" (Rom. 3:26).

After examining our lost and hopeless condition *without* Christ, can anyone who is IN Christ deny that he has been *forgiven much*? Does God have different brands of salvation . . . one for a very immoral woman and another for a moral, self-righteous church member? No, being good does not change the perfection nor the degree of salvation. Jesus shed His blood and died on the cross *for everyone*, and through His shed blood we ALL have a *perfect* salvation. "For by one offering He hath perfected for ever them that are sanctified" (Heb. 10:14).

The sinner in the gutter–the miserable wretch who is loved by no one–need not despair because of his hopeless condition, for God *can* and *will save* him, if that sinner will come to God. "Wherefore He is able also to save them to the uttermost that come unto God by Him . . ." (Heb. 7:25). The morally upright sinner need not have the false notion that he is "not so bad" and that he needs little forgiveness, for "without the shedding of blood is NO remission," and without a sense of having sinned he will not call upon God for salvation. If there is no real sense of sin, then there will be no repentance – and God's Word says, ". . . Except ye *repent*, ye shall all likewise perish" (Luke 13:3). "Godly sorrow worketh repentance to salvation . . ." (II Cor. 7:10). Without salvation, the sinner is doomed to an eternal, burning hell. His goodness cannot save him nor *help* save him. ("All our righteousnesses are as filthy rags" (Isa. 64:6).

Christ died but once . . . and it takes the same sacrificial death of Christ to save the moral person that it takes to save the wicked, mean, immoral person.

In closing, let me ask you a direct question: *Where do you stand NOW*? Have you accepted Christ as your Saviour, and therefore you stand "NOT CONDEMNED"? Or have you rejected the Saviour–and stand before a holy, righteous God, "CONDEMNED NOW"?

Answer that question – and if in your heart you

recognize yourself as a sinner, I trust you will also recognize that without Christ there is no hope for you. God in His mercy has left you among the living, and through this message He is calling you again . . . giving you another chance. The rejected blood still cries, "COME!" The door of access to the mercy of God is still open for you. Will you heap sin upon sin . . . judgment upon judgment . . . by refusing to come? God forbid! May this be the day you come to Jesus . . . and from this day onward go on your way rejoicing that your sins which were many are all washed away!

Christian, if you have ever entertained the thought that you were not so bad, and therefore God forgave you *little*, may you repent of your self-righteousness . . . and from this day onward thank God for, and rejoice in, the fact that He has forgiven you . . . MUCH!

BE SURE YOUR SIN WILL FIND YOU OUT

BE SURE YOUR SIN WILL FIND YOU OUT

"Yet they were not afraid, nor rent their garments, neither the king, nor any of his servants that heard all these words" (Jer. 36:24).

Jeremiah brought message after message of warning from God to His people, messages in which their sins were named and judgments pronounced. Over and over again in the book of Jeremiah we find these words: *"Then the Word of the Lord came unto me, saying . . . ."* Even though his message was directly from God, the people did not repent. They seemed to forget or ignore the divine warnings, in spite of the fact that they were repeated over and over again.

So God adopted another method of warning His people: ". . . This word came unto Jeremiah from the Lord, saying, Take thee a roll of a book, and write therein all the words that I have spoken unto thee against Israel, and against Judah, and against all nations, from the day I spake unto thee, from the days of Josiah, even unto this day. It may be that the house of Judah will hear all the evil which I purpose to do unto them; that they may return every man from his evil way; that I may forgive their iniquity and their sin" (Jer. 36:1–3).

This Scripture reminds us of another verse, found in the New Testament: "The Lord is . . . longsuffering to us-ward, not willing that any should perish, but that all should come to repentance" (II Pet. 3:9).

God does everything possible to keep men out of hell and to bring His own children to repentance. He was long-suffering with Judah in the days of Jeremiah, and tried in many ways to bring them to repentance. It would seem that the method of writing *in one book* all the words spoken against Judah would bring about results. Though the warnings, threatenings, and revelations of God had made no impression upon the hearers when delivered separately, with intervals between, yet it might be hoped that if they were presented all at one time, written down in a book, they would be more effective. According to God's command, these warnings *were* all written down and were read—first to the people, and afterward to the king and his princes.

We need only to read the prophecy of Jeremiah to know that it was one of the most alarming, heart-rending messages ever sent from God to man—such verses as the following:

Jeremiah 6:11,12: "Therefore I am full of the fury of the Lord; I am weary with holding in: I will pour it out upon the children abroad, and upon the assembly of young men together: for even the husband with the wife shall be taken, the aged with him that is full of days. And their houses shall be turned unto others, with their fields and wives together: for I will stretch out my hand upon the inhabitants of the land, saith the Lord."

Jeremiah 9:16: "I will scatter them also among the heathen, whom neither they nor their fathers have known: and I will send a sword after them, till I have consumed them."

Jeremiah 7:16: "Therefore pray not thou for this people, neither lift up cry nor prayer for them, neither make intercession to me: for I will not hear thee."

Jeremiah 7:20: "Therefore thus saith the Lord God; Behold, mine anger and my fury shall be poured out upon this place, upon man, and upon beast, and upon the trees of the field, and upon the fruit of the ground; and it shall burn, and shall not be quenched."

The warnings of Jeremiah were messages of such utter destruction and almighty vengeance that had the people believed, the warnings were enough to chill the blood and freeze the soul with horror. Yet at the same time, those messages contained such tender invitations to repentance, such wonderful assurances of God's willingness to forgive, one wonders how the people could ignore them: "Return, ye backsliding children, and I will heal your backslidings. Behold, we come unto thee; for thou art the Lord our God" (Jer. 3:22).

Yet, when all of these warnings were penned down and read to the people and to the princes, the Bible tells us, "Yet they were not afraid, nor rent their garments!" The phraseology of this plainly intimates that the people should have been afraid and deeply disturbed–but they were not. What else could God do but bring judgment upon them? He warned, He pleaded, He threatened – and He offered mercy; but they turned a deaf ear to Him. Therefore, judgment struck: Jerusalem was captured and the people were carried away into Babylon (Jer. 39).

Many of you will readily agree that God gave these people sufficient warnings and ample opportunity to repent. You will agree that He was justified in administering the judgment He had threatened. Yet, in your admission of this, *you condemn yourself*! God is pursuing *you*, and for a long time He has been using the same method with you that He employed with Judah–with no results. The same God who spoke to Judah by His prophet has, in these latter times, spoken to YOU by *His Son*–nor is that all: In His Book He has recorded His love, His provisions, His warnings–and His judgments.

In the Gospels He has set before us the judgments of a divine God who cannot condone nor look upon sin (Matt. 25:41; 10:33; John 3:36; Mark 9:43). He has recorded invitations and offers of mercy far more tender, proofs of His love far more powerful, than He ever offered to His ancient people. He has brought life and immortality more clearly to light, the veil has been rent asunder, and any and all may enter into the holy of holies. The glories of heaven have been made more real and the flames of hell have been unveiled before our eyes on the pages of Holy Writ.

In fact, all that God has done and all that He *will do* has been recorded in our Bible. We are sinners bound for an eternal hell, God has provided salvation to keep us out of that hell, and these solemn facts are penned down for all to read. This was done with the same end in view as was the record Jeremiah wrote – it was done that we as sinners might read it, be convicted of our sins, and through the atonement of Jesus Christ *be saved.*

Even those of you who have not read the Scriptures are to some extent acquainted with the message of love and the message of divine judgment, for you have heard it preached and taught since you were a child. Some of you have heard–and been saved; others have heard in vain –and, as in Jeremiah's day, *you are not ashamed nor alarmed.* You consider that your position is different from that of ancient Judah. You understand that you must either be saved or perish, and you think you will not do as others have done but will make your peace with God before it is too late. "There is time," you say–but right now you are not ready.

You–and thousands of others like you–soothe your conscience by saying that you are morally good and you attend church–but you will not heed God's warning that "Except a man be born again, he cannot see the kingdom of God" (John 3:3). Romans 6:23: "*The wages of sin is death.*" James 1:15: ". . . *Sin, when it is finished, bringeth forth death.*"

With reverence I call upon the insulted Majesty of heaven to witness the manner in which His declarations are received—and the little effect they produce! How many sinners do you know who are stirred enough by them to ask, "*What shall I do to be saved*?" Sinners are not one-tenth as concerned over God's warnings as they are over a trip to the moon, nor are they as affected by God's divine threatenings as they would be by a rumor of an invasion by men from Mars!

It is enormous, heaven-provoking wickedness to hear God's Word without any emotion; it is a sin that expresses the utmost contempt for God. The man who without fear hears God's commands, expresses contempt for God; one who hears His tender invitation, "Come unto me, and I will give you rest . . . Believe on the Lord Jesus Christ, and thou shalt be saved," and ignores those invitations, is insulting Almighty God. This is the *greatest* of insults, and is offered to God ten thousand times over again every day.

Will God allow these sinners to get by? Will He wink at these insults? No! It is recorded in His Word, "*Be not deceived; God is not mocked: for whatsoever a man soweth, that shall he also reap*" (Gal. 6:7). ". . . For there is nothing covered, that shall not be revealed; and hid, that shall not be known. What I tell you in darkness, that speak ye in light: and what ye hear in the ear, that preach ye upon the housetops" (Matt. 10:26,27).

Highest Degree of Unbelief

Those who hear the Word and pay no attention to it, in effect call God a liar. If they really believed in an eternal hell with fire and brimstone, and that they are bound for hell because they are not saved; if they really believed that there is a Saviour who died for them and who will save them if they will only accept His finished work, they would accept Christ without having to be begged to do so – IF they only believed! The trouble is that they do not really *believe* that they are lost, miserable, hell-bound sinners. They say, "Such messages are for murderers, harlots, dopers, and despicable characters of the underworld–not for us." They neither admit nor recognize that they are lost. They will not admit that their deeds are evil. They think they are all right as long as they keep their sins hidden from others, and they make excuses, trying to justify their actions to themselves. But all of their excuses are no good. In the days of old, God did not let the people of Judah get by – and the people of today will not get by with ignoring God's warnings and His love! "*Be sure your sin will find you out!*" (Num. 32:23).

The people who heard Jeremiah's warnings said, "This evil will not come upon us" (Jer. 5:12). They were "at ease in Zion" (Amos 6:1), because they thought their sins were hidden from God and that He was not going to do anything about it! Some of YOU are just as hard-hearted and just as foolish. Because you have gotten by with your sin for years and nothing has happened to you, you say, "God's Word does not mean what it says!" You are not afraid, and many of you prosper. Many keep their sins hidden from man for a long time – and seemingly God has overlooked their sinfulness; but watch out! God cannot lie! Your sin will find you out; it will catch up with you.

Hard-Hearted

Those who hear the Word of God without being affected by it display extreme hardness of heart–and the more they hear His Word and ignore His warnings, the harder and more unimpressive their hearts become. The sin of hardening the heart to God's warnings will swiftly bring destruction: "He, that being often reproved hardeneth his neck, shall suddenly be destroyed, and that without remedy!" (Prov. 29:1).

If you have trouble believing that a loving God will deal in judgment, look for example at the OLD world. It was corrupt, filled with violence, and every imagination of the thoughts of man's heart was evil (Gen. 6:5). Yet God was patient, for the people had not yet heard His message with *indifference.* God's patience then ended—for Noah, a preacher of righteousness, warned them; but they were indifferent to his warnings, they would not repent, they were not alarmed. Why? *Because they did not believe Noah's message.* This unbelief sealed their doom, and the flood came upon them and destroyed them all.

Consider the Jews in our Saviour's time here on earth. They were religious—but lost; they *professed much*, but the majority of them were very wicked, even immoral (John 8:9–11). And yet all of their sins were as nothing when compared to their hearing Jesus with unconcern and unbelief! Our Saviour said, "*If I had not come and spoken unto them, they had not had sin: but now they have no cloke for their sin*" (John 15:22). The history of the Jews stands as a monument to the truth of God's Word: *Judgment struck*! The Jew has suffered as no other nation has ever suffered, and those Jews who died in unbelief went to hell.

Sinner friend, do you think YOU will get by? Hear God when He says, "*Be sure your sin will find you out*!" Hear this with concern, belief, and alarm. Sin will not only catch up with you, bringing divine judgment, but that sin will also be brought to light!

Why is it impossible to keep sin covered and ungodly acts concealed? It is impossible *because God says so* —

and even had He NOT said so, through the weakness of the flesh the sinner would soon give himself away. When a person first does wrong, he is very cautious–and through the conviction of his conscience he is repentant. But as time goes on his heart hardens; he is no longer careful and even indulges in deeper and deeper sin. He becomes careless in his sins, perhaps thinking he is getting by–but not so! Those who hear God's Word with unconcern become hard-hearted, careless, and then comes to pass what God's Word thunders out: "BE SURE YOUR SIN WILL FIND YOU OUT!"

Sin is deceiving. Little by little, a person is lured deeper and deeper into the very thing he plans to quit eventually. The cords of sin twine about him and bind him so tightly that only God can set him free. Never fool yourself into thinking that you are going to quit your special secret sin before you are found out. Every derelict, drunkard, disgraced and unhappy person started out that way, never dreaming they would end up on the human junk-pile.

Not long ago a man came to my husband so disturbed he was ready to take his own life. He worked with an attractive young woman, and they began a flirtation "on a small scale." He said he really loved his wife and never intended this flirtation to amount to anything. He began taking the girl out and telling his wife lies about where he was going–all of the time intending to drop the girl and quit deceiving his wife before the affair went too far. But he could find no stopping place–and when he wanted to stop, the girl would not let him. His wife then found out, and all that was dear to his heart slipped from him.

Some people are caught in the very beginning of their deceit. They should be thankful for this, rather than being resentful. Behind such a person there must be a praying mother or loved one. If the man just mentioned had been seen by his wife the first time he went out with the girl, there might have been some words between them—but not a separation. A traveler has no room to complain if he loses a leg at the beginning of his journey, thereby preventing the loss of his *head* at the *end* of it!

There are many girls who were tempted to indulge in some sinful act, but who, as a brand, were snatched from the fire. They were seen or found out before they actually indulged, and were so frightened it kept them from attempting such a thing again. A little scorching kept them from falling into the fire; but this is not always the case. The devil makes it easy to start out in sin, and there are all too few mothers and fathers who pray for their children.

Perhaps you have been successful thus far in keeping your sin hidden—but that does not mean that you can continue to do so. Regardless of how carefully you try to cover your sinful indulgences, eventually you will become careless, or some unforeseen circumstance will uncover your lies. God has ways and means you could never think of. A husband who deceives his wife will be suddenly and unmercifully shown up. His wife may think he is "out with the boys"—when his deceit is suddenly brought to light by a terrible car wreck. Girls who tell their mothers they are going one place, and go to another, will eventually meet with some accident through which their sin will be brought to light. There are church members who for years have hidden a mean, selfish, covetous heart—but in some unguarded moment it is made plain before the whole church. Girls who live sinful lives while posing as virtuous, innocent girls will be brought low when their shame can no longer be hidden.

Sinner, "Be sure YOUR sin will find you out"—in

hell, if not before! "The wages of sin is death." You may get by your fellowman, but *you cannot hide from God.* Throughout eternity you will reap for your wicked life. You may fool your family, even your pastor (if you have one); but you will never fool God. The very God you are trying to ignore has supplied a means of escape. "God so loved the world, that He gave His only begotten Son, that whosoever believeth in Him should not perish, but have everlasting life" (John 3:16).

You can come to Jesus and have your sins forgiven, removed from you as far as the east is from the west, to be remembered against you no more; but you cannot reject God's Son, spurn His matchless love, *and get by*! Why not accept Jesus Christ right now and let Him put all those wicked sins under His blood? He will hide them forever.

Some of you are tormented because of the life you live. Your conscience condemns you, and peace is something unknown to your soul. What a blessed relief to accept Christ, let Him take that burden of sin away, and cleanse you whiter than the snow! The peace of God cannot be purchased with money, but it is yours for the taking—it is the gift of God. Why carry your burden and your load of sin any longer? Christ bore your sin on the cross: "He was wounded for our transgressions, He was bruised for our iniquities: the chastisement of our peace was upon Him; and with His stripes we are healed. . . the Lord hath laid on Him the iniquity of us all" (Isa. 53:5,6).

To Christians:

While it is true that impenitent *sinners* hear the Word with unconcern, as did Judah, it is also true that many *professed believers* who used to tremble at the divine threatenings of the Lord now cease to be concerned at all. To many, the messages of God on hell, heaven, judgment, and eternity have almost become just so many idle words. They excite no joy and produce no fear in the hearts of these people.

God's Word says, "If we confess our sins, He is faithful and just to forgive us our sins, and to cleanse us from all unrighteousness" (I John 1:9). I Corinthians 11: 31,32 tells us, "If we would judge ourselves, we should not be judged. But when we are judged, we are chastened of the Lord, that we should not be condemned with the world." God gave us this record in His holy Book for the same reason the warnings of Jeremiah were given; but many of you–though you have read the warnings and the promises–have not been affected by them. You act in the same manner as did the princes of Judah. You have not been alarmed, you are not alarmed even now – but just as surely as judgment fell upon the Jews, it will fall upon YOU. God's chastening hand is raised, and your chastening is inevitable. I Corinthians 11:30 says, "For this cause many are weak and sickly among you, and many sleep." In I John 5:16 we are told, ". . . *There is a sin unto death*!"

Christian, you cannot continue to ignore God's warnings and get away with it. "*Be sure your sin will find you out.*" There are many ways in this life that sin will find you out, but the main loss to a child of God is his loss of reward (I Cor. 3:11 ff).

John pleads with the children of God to "Look to yourselves, that we lose not those things which we have wrought, but that we receive a FULL REWARD" (II John 8). Watch yourself. Be careful! Do not let the devil steal your reward! I do not know what it will be like to be in heaven without a reward, but the Bible clearly teaches that such a thing can happen. God forbid that it happen to you or to me, dear Christian.

If you have become careless, if you are dabbling in sin, STOP! Repent, and renew your vows to God–NOW! "Return ye now–every one–from his evil way, and make your ways and your doings good" (Jer. 18:11b).

There is no need to argue with God's Word. His Word is forever settled in heaven and it will not change. He says: "BE SURE (no guesswork, no way of escape) YOUR SIN WILL FIND YOU OUT!"

I have tried to sound a warning for careless Christians. God's child cannot play with sin and get away with it. Christian, be warned from His Word. *Obey* His Word, and you will have a happy, fruitful Christian life and receive a FULL REWARD at the end of life's journey. *Be sure*–young or old, married or single, sinner or saint–*your sin will find you out*!

To the sinner I say, Bring your sins to Jesus this moment, let Him put them under the blood and remember them against you no more. "The blood of Jesus Christ, God's Son, cleanseth . . . from ALL sin" (I John 1:7). When your sin is under the blood, God forgets that you have ever sinned. You are just as pure in God's sight as the blood that covers your sin.

THE ENEMY WITHIN

THE ENEMY WITHIN

There are *three powerful evils* which work from within us to hinder our spiritual growth and progress. It is my intention to discuss these evils briefly, hoping to help someone who has not been *aware* of these deadly evils working from within.

Bitterness:

"*. . . Lest any root of bitterness springing up trouble you, and thereby many be defiled*" (Heb. 12:15). Notice that the Word says "*root* of bitterness," implying something more than a passing fancy or temporary passion. "*Root*" indicates that the bitterness goes deep into the soul, a condition deeply and firmly implanted. Bitterness is not just an ingrafted branch or leaves that can easily be cut off, but a *root* which has taken a firm hold and is difficult to be rid of.

Romans 11:16 says, ". . . If the *root* be holy, so are the branches." Therefore we might say that if the "root of bitterness" is in the soul, "so is *the whole nature* of that person."

One drop of ink in a glass of clear water discolors the whole glass. Just so, the root of bitterness discolors, warps, and influences the whole being. There are many things which cause bitterness, but the *results* can all be classified under *two headings.*

The *first* of these–though perhaps not the most frequent–is *bitterness toward God.* God sometimes has to deal with His children in chastisement, and because of the chastisement some become bitter and complain against Him. They think He has not dealt fairly with them and that He has put more upon them than He has put upon anyone else. They continually ask, "Why did God let this happen to ME?" They cannot see that God has allowed this particular thing to happen for their own good and for His glory. Therefore, because of their spiritual blindness, they think they have been unjustly treated by God, and bitterness against Him takes root in their hearts.

Secondly—and more frequently—people become *bitter toward their fellowman.* Someone treats them unkindly or does them an injustice, and immediately the root of bitterness springs up. The sad, sad fact is that most people are not willing to make things right. They say, "I was treated unjustly, and the person who did it is fully aware of it! The situation cannot be made right." Bitterness has so distorted their outlook on life that they cannot observe the situation in its true perspective. They let bitterness grow until it dominates every phase of their being, and those around them even recognize bitterness in their *speech* . . . it is what they constantly talk about and argue about.

When it is suggested to such a person that he go to the other party and talk the matter over, he immediately says, "It is no use! I would not believe anything he (or she) says. Actions speak louder than words."

My! But it is sad when a person does not want to make things right with others, and then attempts to justify such bitterness by saying, "I am only human, and I have been terribly mistreated. I have suffered a terrible wrong!" Yes, you are still suffering—not directly from the wrong, but from the bitterness which you are harboring in your heart. This is a terrible kind of suffering, and it "eateth at the heart as a cancer."

Nine times out of ten, this bitterness arises between

brethren in the church or between members of a family. It is much easier to overlook the wrong-doings of a downright sinner or an enemy, than to overlook that of a close relative or a fellow church member—because the hurt goes deeper when a professing Christian, a fellow church member, or a relative does you an injustice. But *Jesus Christ* "came unto His own, and *His own received Him not.*" Another Scripture says, "What are these wounds in thine hands? Then He shall answer, Those with which I was wounded *in the house of my friends*" (Zech. 13:6).

But then you readily say, "I am only human, and I cannot be like Jesus, who was the Son of God." No, but you can allow Jesus to do for you what you cannot do for yourself. He can uproot the bitterness and throw it out. The whole trouble is that you *are not willing* . . . you do not intend to attempt to remove the bitterness. You are determined to keep the grudge. You would not be pleased, even if the person were found to be innocent of the charge which you have made against him. No, your mind is made up to the fact that he has done wrong and, to a certain extent, you get satisfaction out of being bitter toward him!

The Bible says, "If thy brother shall trespass against thee, go and tell him his fault between thee and him alone: if he shall hear thee, thou hast gained thy brother" (Matt. 18:15). Very few are willing to do this. They will say, "It would not be of any use . . . the damage is done now, and it cannot be repaired." Maybe not, but one thing can be changed: That bitterness can be dug out by the roots and cast out of your heart and life. This digging-out process can come only by the grace and power of God. You yourself do not have to have the power, but you have to be willing for God to do the digging. If you are sincerely willing in your desire for God to remove the bitterness from your heart, then He will do it. He is greater than the devil, and His power is unlimited in the heart of one who is willing for God to have His way. If I did not think God could work a miracle and remove all bitterness from the human heart and life, then I would not have much confidence in my God! But I KNOW that He *can* and that He WILL work such a miracle in your heart if you are *willing* for Him to do so. My — what a burden will roll from your heart once you turn it all over to Jesus!

In the long run, you who are bitter are the losers. Bitterness and hatred make you unhappy and affect your whole life—especially your *spiritual* life. You have been wronged by someone and have suffered from the deed, but a thousand times more you are suffering now from the bitterness in your own heart. *It is not worth it*!

Some have said, "Even though I *forgave* the person, I could never have the confidence in him and the love for him that I once had." All right . . . just be *neutral* and allow God to uproot the bitterness and cast it out. Forgive the person, and you will find that you can then think of that person with no ill feeling at all. You may not think of him with the affection and the love which you once had—but a good clean, healthy feeling toward him is far better and sweeter to the soul than the hatred which you now have. I sincerely believe that in time God will heal the wound and you will be able to go on your way rejoicing.

The root of bitterness is an evil thing. It is dividing churches and breaking up homes. Please let me warn some of you who have bitterness toward your fellow church member: Be *sure* that you have been wronged, in the first place. I have seen so many people carrying grudges, who only *thought* they had been treated wrongly. The way things looked, they had a right to be angry with the other person;

but in some cases, I have known that "other person" and I know the accusation was unjust. That person was innocent. Are you honestly sure and positive that someone has done you a wrong? Or are you just going by what you *heard* or what you *think*? You had better be sure. You will have to give an account to God one of these days. In the meantime, you are letting bitterness rob you of your joy. How can you honestly kneel and pray with that unforgiveness in your heart? Ephesians 4:32 tells us, "And be ye kind one to another, tenderhearted, *forgiving one another, even as God for Christ's sake hath forgiven you.*"

When the Israelites were traveling from Egypt to the Promised Land, they were at one time suffering from the lack of water. When they *did* find water, they could not drink it because it was bitter. There was water, and it was wet . . . the people were thirsty—but they could not drink it. How true in the lives of many Christians. God cannot use them because they are bitter; they have the message, and the world is thirsty for that message – but the world cannot drink at a bitter fountain.

"And when they came to Marah, they could not drink of the waters of Marah, for they were bitter: therefore the name of it was called Marah" (Ex. 15:23). The next verse tells us that the people began to murmur against Moses. Moses cried unto the Lord, and the Lord showed him a tree. But what good could a tree do to help sweeten bitter water? Moses did not question the Lord, but rather *obeyed* Him by casting the tree into the bitter waters—and the water was made SWEET! The tree which God showed Moses represented the Cross on which the Lamb of God was to die . . . the Cross which, when applied, will sweeten bitter souls and lives.

It does not matter how bitter you have become . . . you,

too, can become sweet in the soul if you will let the "Tree" occupy the heart of your very being. There is power in the Blood – and only through the power of the Cross and the blood Jesus shed there, can the bitter become sweet.

Care:

"*Casting all your care upon Him; for He careth for you*" (I Pet. 5:7). Care chokes the development of the inner life. People who worry are not trusting. A fretful, worried person cannot grow in grace.

In the parable of the Sower we are told that the thorny-ground hearers are they who are "*choked with cares* and riches and pleasures of this life, and bring no fruit to perfection" (Luke 8:14).

This can be applied to God's people. How often the work of the Spirit is hindered in a person's heart because that heart is weighed down with the cares of the world! Many mothers are weighed down with the cares of the home. They cannot buy new curtains, or they cannot keep the house as immaculately clean as they desire. The matter of clothes (or the lack of new ones) keeps them worried and dissatisfied. The grocery bill is high, and the laundry is exceedingly large. Erelong these cares will choke the grace of patience, and a nervous, ill-tempered wife and mother is the result. This undue concern does not make the grocery bill less, nor put new curtains at the windows. I am sure the rest of the family would rather have a kind, loving, patient mother, than to have all the luxuries of life.

There is certainly nothing wrong in being concerned over the household matters . . . it is the mother's duty to see after these things; but it does not help to *worry and fret* – nor does God excuse a person for doing so. It is against His direct command. His Word says: "Be careful for nothing; but in every thing by prayer and supplication with thanksgiving let your requests be made known unto God" (Phil. 4:6). "*Be careful for nothing*" . . . in other words, "In nothing be anxious." But you say, "How am I to obey such a command when my troubles are pressing sorely upon me?" God's Word points the way.

He would have you to bring everything to Him . . . the great things and the little things, the trying experiences . . . and *leave them there.* You may feel that you do not know the mind of the Lord in regard to your troubles–but regardless of that, take them to Him and LEAVE THEM THERE. You are to make known your requests, counting on His wisdom to do for you that which is best for time and eternity. Thus, casting all your care upon Him and leaving all in His own blessed hands, the peace of God shall flood your soul and "shall keep your hearts and minds through Christ Jesus."

A sweet, loving, kind mother is better to give to your family than are new clothes, new furniture, and the finest of foods.

Many young girls are so weighted down with care and selfishness that they make life miserable for others, just because they cannot have all the fine things they want. Young lady, the cares of social life will choke the *plant of separation* in a Christian's heart. The desire to be popular and to have a good time is a thorny bush which will grow up in your life, causing you to compromise with the world. Erelong you will find yourself unhappy, unfruitful, and far away from the Lord. Some of you girls are worried because you are not invited into certain groups and clubs! You are so ambitious to obtain this social status that you are even scheming and planning and worrying over a way to be invited. You would thank God that you are NOT invited, if your reasoning and your spiritual sight were not choked with care for the social life! In most of these clubs and groups, you would have to deny your Lord if you DID get into them.

There are many other ways in which girls are permitting the cares of the world to choke out their spiritual growth and usefulness. Any young lady who does not have the joy of her salvation need only check up and, if she is really honest, she can immediately find the "why." Young lady, are you weighted down with some care of this world, whether it be pleasures, clothes, or friends? God knows all about it—and *He cares*! Cast "all your care upon Him; for He careth for you."

The cares of business life will choke the prayer and Bible study from a life. Every man should try to make a comfortable living for his family; but he is not to put business and money-making before God. Many a man sits up late and gets up early, to make an extra dollar. He may be successful in business, but *he is losing out with God.* Bible study is neglected, and he cannot find time to pray! His business occupies his mind and his time. He is so weighed down with the cares of his business, and so worried about making an extra dollar, that the thorns of covetousness and pride grow fast in his heart, and choke out his spiritual growth and fruitfulness. Of course, to ease his conscience, he gives liberally to the church – but the giving of his money is not like giving *himself.* Giving money to the church does not feed his soul . . . neither does it answer for his lack of prayer.

The Word of God says: "Behold, to obey is better than sacrifice, and to hearken than the fat of rams" (I Sam. 15:22). Your gifts may be large – but if you are not obeying God in first giving yourself, and if you are not devoting some of your time to Bible study and prayer, then you are not pleasing God. "Seek ye *first* the kingdom of God, and His righteousness; and all these things shall be added unto you" (Matt. 6:33).

Care is a robber: It robs us of time which we should be giving to Christ . . . if we are *trusting*, then we are not *worrying*. *Martha* was rebuked by Christ for being careful about many things (Luke 10:41). Martha was so full of care that she had no time to sit at the Master's feet and listen to His word. She was in a turmoil and was very upset. In her condition she was not actually *fit* to take in the words of Christ, even if she had taken a few minutes to listen. How true of hundreds of Christians today! They go to church with their minds in a whirl, worried over one thing or another–and even though they sit through a sermon they never hear a word. Their worries and their cares have robbed them of spiritual food!

Martha even tried to get Christ to rebuke Mary because *she* was not worried about preparing dinner. Those who are blinded with care are sure to see faults in others. They are ready to criticize anyone who is at peace with God and who has the peace of God abiding in his heart. It makes them angry to see someone else happy – yet it is their own fault that they themselves are so miserable. I suppose that among the most pitiful are those people who are so cumbered with the care of church activities . . . church suppers, outings, and programs. They are so cumbered that they are unhappy, and they resent anyone else who IS happy. Christ desires the love of the heart before the labor of the hands. When He has the first, the second is sure to follow.

Care shuts out the Lord. He has given us loving directions for our cares: "Casting all your care upon Him;

for He careth for you." Our Lord is surely grieved when we shut Him out and continue to be cumbered with care. Why not trust Him with the burdens and the cares of this life? He knows every heartache and every desire. He sees the little sparrow when it falls. How much more He loves *you*, for whom He shed His precious blood!

Some of the things which you now want may not be best for you. Do not worry and fret over it. Lean heavily upon Him who is our Burden Bearer. Some of you have spent hours and days worrying over a certain matter–and, to your surprise, when the thing really happened, you discovered that there was really nothing at all to worry about! Just trust Christ, and He will work everything out for your good and for His glory. He wants you to trust Him . . . and not to worry and fret.

Cowardice:

No one likes to be called a coward. It is certainly an insult. Yet many of God's children are nothing short of cowards.

In II Peter 1:5 we read, "And beside this, giving all diligence, add to your faith *virtue* (*courage, strength*); and to virtue knowledge." *Cowardice cripples a testimony.* The one thing which impressed the rulers, causing them to "sit up and take notice," was the *courage* of the early Christians. Those Christians stood up and confessed Christ in the face of death, torment, and punishment. "Now when they saw the *boldness* of Peter and John, and perceived that they were unlearned and ignorant men, they marvelled; and they took knowledge of them, that they had been with Jesus" (Acts 4:13).

In Rome some Christians were fed to the lions, while others were used as human torches when they refused to deny the Lord. But where did they get this courage and power? There is only one answer: *From the Lord*! The Holy Spirit had complete control of their hearts and lives; therefore the weak became strong, and fear was replaced by courage.

It is a person's own fault if he is too much of a coward to testify and to stand up for the Lord. God will give the needed boldness and courage to those who really *want* Him to do so. It requires only a complete yielding to Christ and a sincere desire to please *Him* before pleasing self or others. Many people want to be saved in order that they may escape hell – but they do not want to go any further. They do not want their salvation to *cost* them anything . . . they are *cowards*. Indeed, they are poor advertisement for Christ. These Christians need to take another look at the Cross.

The great, sacrificial death of Jesus Christ was necessary in order that you and I, wretched lost sinners, might be saved. He who was sinless became sin. He who was life, died that we might live. He who took our place and suffered in our stead has not asked us to die on a cross nor to be spit upon and beaten with many stripes. He has only asked us to love Him with all of our hearts, and to acknowledge Him before men. Is that asking too much? What a coward a person is, who will deny the precious Saviour! When a man betrays his best friend, it is said of him that he is a "dirty coward." How much *lower* a person is, who has accepted the great salvation and has benefited by the sufferings and death of Christ, and then denies Him before an evil and an adulterous people!

The *Holy Spirit* will supply the power and the courage. You do not have to be strong. Fall completely in love with Jesus, and you will never deny Him.

If you are a coward concerning your testimony, it will DAMPEN THE LOVE FOR SOULS IN YOUR HEART. Love for souls will burn brightly on the altar of the heart if it is fed with the fuel of God's love. But cowardice is like water poured on that fire. It smothers the zeal for the lost and discourages any Christlike service to others.

Cowardice was the cause of Peter's denial of the Lord. It had so chilled his heart that the flame of love was smothered, and he denied his Lord while trying to save his own neck! Not a pretty picture – but many who are just as guilty as Peter was, are ready to criticize and condemn him.

Peter went out and wept in repentance, and later he stood up for the crucified Christ, in the face of death. We are told that he, too, was crucified, and that he asked to be crucified up-side-down . . . realizing, no doubt, that he was not worthy to be crucified in the same manner as was his Lord. Yes, Peter once had a heart filled with cowardice (and that is a black mark against his name), but later he had spiritual stamina which would equal that of any man.

Peter repented – but some of *you* are *still cowards.* Of course, you do not call it by that name . . . you say, "I don't think a person should advertise his religion and act like a fanatic." Or you say, "There is a time and a place for all things." That kind of reasoning may sound very well on the surface – but if you let God have complete control of your life, you will not speak out of place . . . and neither will you keep your mouth shut and deny your Lord. Romans 8:14 says: "For as many as are led by the Spirit of God, they are the sons of God." Or, we could say that the sons of God are *led by the Spirit of God.*

I hesitate to mention this, but it seems necessary.

People are wondering why so many preachers who have preached the Word are *now compromising* and selling out to the denominations. It is nothing short of *cowardice.* They are afraid they will lose their churches . . . afraid the ministerial association will kick them out, and then they will be unable to find a place to preach. Oh . . . if we only had more preachers like Paul! On one occasion he said, ". . . No man stood with me, but all men forsook me . . . Notwithstanding THE LORD STOOD WITH ME—AND STRENGTHENED ME . . ." (II Tim. 4:16,17). No minister, no Christian, need fear if Christ is with him. When you stand for Christ, He will stand by you. What a comfort!

Cowardice before men (being afraid of what they can do to you) *shows lack of confidence toward God.* "Beloved, if our heart condemn us not, then have we confidence toward God" (I John 3:21). If we—preachers, deacons, mothers, fathers, or children—can look into the face of God with confidence, then we can look into the face of *any man* with courage. If a preacher is kicked out of one church for his uncompromising stand for God, then God has a better door standing ajar and ready for him to enter. When the man who was healed of his blindness in John 9 was cast out of the temple, Jesus was right there, ready to lift him up, to encourage him, and to assure him of eternal life.

Cowardice also discourages prayer. Those who truly want to stand true to the Lord will seek His aid in prayer. But those who are cowards will not ask Him for courage. The prayer life of a coward dwindles to almost nothing. How it must grieve the heart of the Lord when one of His children turns coward and traitor, and in action or words denies Him! *He* is not ashamed to call us *brethren* — therefore why should we be ashamed to own Him as Lord of all?

The task may be difficult and the enemy strong. Men may be against us and the devil always on the job to discourage us – but in the face of all this and *above* it all, we can hear our blessed Lord saying: "Be not afraid."

"I am with you alway, even unto the end of the world" (Matt. 28:20).

"I will never leave thee, nor forsake thee. So that we may BOLDLY say, The Lord is my helper, and I will not fear what man shall do unto me" (Heb. 13:5,6).

I beg you who name the name of Christ, let us put away all cowardice and at all costs be true to the Lord, true to His Word, and true to His love by loving others.

I Peter 2:2 says, "As newborn babes, desire the sincere milk of the Word, that ye may grow thereby." Do you really wish to grow in grace and to win souls to Christ? Then take an inventory of your life, and see whether any of the things which I have mentioned are hindering your growth. Are you really happy in the Lord? If you are not, perhaps you are letting the enemy of the soul rob you of that joy by encouraging you to hold on to your bitterness, care, or cowardice. It is true that we are told in the Word of God to "grow in grace"–but the verse which precedes I Peter 2:2 says: "Wherefore *laying aside* all malice, and all guile, and hypocrisies, and envies, and all evil speakings."

Those thorny bushes must be dug up and cast out of the heart before there can be any spiritual growth. I sincerely pray that you have been made to think, and that you will determine in your heart to let God do a little pruning and digging in your life–that you, too, may "grow in grace."

WHAT'S WRONG WITH ME?

WHAT'S WRONG WITH ME?

"These things write we unto you, that your joy may be full" (I John 1:4).

"What is wrong in my Christian life?" This is an earnest question asked by many Christians. On examination of the lives of others, they notice there is a manifestation of joy and peace which they themselves do not always possess. "Oh, that I might only have the power, victory and joy that others have in their Christian life!" is a constant heart-cry of many. It is well to be dissatisfied with the low levels of Christian living, and I would never encourage anyone to be content with a half-hearted Christian life. . . but many times this dissatisfaction arises not from the fact that something is wrong with the Christian—but that he *does not understand* many things pertaining to his spiritual life.

In trying to find what is wrong in your Christian life, you must remember that people are basically different. We must never forget that temperaments differ. Some people are born with a sunny disposition . . . and before they are saved, as well as after they are saved, it is easy for them to be pleasant, happy, and joyful. Others are born with a cold, unemotional disposition which carries over into their Christian life. They cannot help this fact . . . they were born with that nature. A reserved, cold-natured person need not be alarmed because he cannot manifest an outward show of emotion. Of course, salvation changes the cold heart to a warm and loving heart – but the person may not have the ability to show it outwardly, any more than he was able to show his emotions *before* he was saved.

For a naturally reserved, unemotional person to force outward manifestations of emotion is to play the hypocrite. After all, it is not the outward show that counts, but the inward condition of the heart.

The first thing a Christian needs to understand is that salvation is of the *heart*—that the "inner man" changes—but the basic personality is the same after salvation as it was before. Therefore, we may safely conclude that an outward show of emotion is no true test of our inward spiritual state.

The absence of joy in the Christian life *may* mean that there is some unconfessed sin in the heart, but this is not always the reason. There are other reasons that sometimes account for the Christian's lack of joy. This could be caused by physical trouble. It may be the nervous system is overtaxed as was Elijah's in the wilderness. After the long strain on Mount Carmel and after his flight was over, Elijah lay down upon the sand and asked that he might die—a request which God answered with food and sleep, rather than with rebuke.

Or perhaps the heart is burdened for the salvation of a lost relative or friend. Under this circumstance, shouting or laughing would be out of place. Patience, courage, and faith are suitable graces to be manifested at such times, rather than outward show of exuberance.

However, when allowance has been made for these and other burdens and cares, it is true that many Christians are missing blessings that are their spiritual birthright, and this loss *may* be traced to something wrong in the Christian life, that should be detected and set right. Here are a few suggestions to help you determine what is wrong:

1. Could it be that you do not recognize your scriptural

position in Christ as distinguished from an emotional experience?

Such experiences are not to be relied upon . . . they are as changing as the weather. You may experience sunshine today, clouds tomorrow; victory today, defeat tomorrow; prayer answered today and no relief from prayer tomorrow. Your *emotional experiences* are ever changing – but your *position in Christ* never changes.

"But of Him *are ye in Christ Jesus*, who of God is made unto us wisdom, and righteousness, and sanctification, and redemption" (I Cor. 1:30). Just what *is* your position? The position of a believer is "IN CHRIST." To be in Him is to be as safe as Noah and his family in the ark were safe from the flood waters. To be in Him is to be as secure as the Israelites were in their blood-sprinkled houses the night of the Passover in Egypt. "For ye are dead, and your life is hid with Christ in God" (Col. 3:3). We are saved, sealed, and secure. Our position in Christ did not originate in us, but in Him and His great love for us. Our position has been purchased by His precious blood–and His blood is just as powerful, is pleading for us just as effectively when we feel our worst as when our faith is strongest and we are at the peak of happiness. Neither doubt nor depression can for a single moment affect or alter our acceptance with God through the blood of Jesus, which acceptance is an eternal fact.

2. Perhaps you live too much in your FEELINGS and too little in your WILL.

We have no direct control over our feelings, but we do have control over our will: "Not *my* will – but *thine* – be done . . . ." God does not hold us responsible for what we feel, but for what we *will*. It is easy to be on the mountain top when in the house of the Lord, feeding on heavenly food – but on the morrow when facing the duties of life, when valley experiences come, the soul is sometimes inclined to question whether it be as consecrated as it formerly was. The Christian is inclined to compare the joy of the mountain-top experience with the difficult walk through the long hours of a working day–and wonder what is wrong. At such a time as this, how glorious it is to know that the WILL has not altered, and in the Christian's heart of hearts his desire is to be as devoted and consecrated in the valley as when enjoying a mountain-top experience.

3. Perhaps you have disobeyed one of God's clear commands.

If you have disobeyed some clear command of God, you know it even now as you read these lines . . . you can distinctly remember it without undue effort in analyzing the past. If you have knowingly disobeyed God, you will know it. If you cannot immediately remember such disobedience, then mark off this possibility and do not spend time worrying and wondering if it exists. For instance, the command could have been a definite "*Go ye,*" and you excused yourself on the grounds of incapability or similar reasons. Or, the command could have been "*Come ye out from among them*"–and you stayed in. You know (and God knows) if you have disobeyed Him. If you have, confess your disobedience–and if it is not too late, obey the command even now. A disobedient child of God need not expect joy, peace, power, and victory. Obey God's clear command, whether it be "Do this," or "Do not do that"–and He will flood your soul with blessings. Walk obediently in the light He has given you, and He will lead you into new paths . . . to greater heights and deeper depths in your Christian life.

4. Perhaps there is some known sin in your life.

In analyzing your Christian life, in trying to find what is wrong, this possibility must be considered – and as in deliberate disobedience, you will immediately recognize this cause of dissatisfaction. Please notice: I said "*known* evil"–something of which God has already convicted you, yet you continue to ignore the conviction and permit this thing to remain in your life. For instance:

Does your will refuse to relinquish a practice or habit which is alien to the will of God?

Do you permit some secret sin to go unconfessed and unjudged in your life?

Do you hold hatred or resentment toward another, and refuse to be reconciled?

Is there some debt you refuse to pay? . . . some honest bill you continue to ignore?

Is there some hurt you refuse to forgive?

Are you allowing something within yourself which you would be quick to condemn in others . . . perhaps excusing yourself on the grounds that in your case it is permissible? Stop and think: Is the frivolous thing you cling to worth the spiritual blessing you have lost by refusing to let it go? I say that *whatever* it is–IT IS NOT WORTH IT!

5. In some instances, the hindrance to blessing is not actual known sin–but WEIGHTS which beset the soul.

Sin is that which is wrong–anywhere, everywhere, with anyone and everyone. *A weight is something that hinders*– or makes Christian growth difficult, without being positively sinful. Some Christians are more easily beset by weights than are others; thus, some Christians are hindered by weights, while others are not. Paul said, "Wherefore seeing we also are compassed about with so great a cloud of witnesses, let us lay aside every *weight*, and the sin which doth so easily beset us, and let us run with patience the race that is set before us" (Heb. 12:1). Each person must decide for himself what constitutes a weight in his life, and what he must lay aside to better fit himself for running the race. If you become fully persuaded in your own mind that there is a weight around your soul, then regardless of how harmless it may be within itself, regardless of how innocently others may be able to allow the same thing in their lives, so far as you are personally concerned there should be no compromise . . . *the weight must go*!

6. Perhaps you look too much INWARD on self, rather than looking UPWARD to the Lord Jesus Christ.

A healthy person will begin to think he is seriously ill if he continually looks for symptoms, counts his heart beat, and diagnoses every imaginary pain. I have known people who have read extensively and talked a great deal on the subject of some particular disease. Before long, they developed every symptom of that disease and were convinced they were in the last stages of it. They went to a doctor and found that X rays and examinations proved they were perfectly sound! Some children of God do exactly as these people do . . . they produce their own doubts and fears by morbid self-examinations. They are always going back to past actions, analyzing them and the motives behind them, worrying over the past. All they ever think of is *self*. When they pray, their prayers are all taken up with condemning self, seeking aid for self.

I would not dare leave the impression that we are not to examine ourselves, or not to judge ourselves. There are times when we definitely should do that. In I Corinthians 11:31 Paul says, "For if we would judge ourselves, we should not be judged." But this self-judgment is for the purpose of making us better Christians with more joy, peace, and victory in our Christian life. When self-judging is over, thank God for forgiveness and go on from there. One does not need to stay forever in such a state. When we judge ourselves and seek God's forgiveness, then we should go on our way rejoicing in the Lord instead of going over and over again things already forgiven. When God forgives – He forgets; why can you not accept that great truth and rejoice in the fact that He is merciful and loving toward you? "Forgetting those things which are behind" is the only safe motto.

A depressed, unhappy, and fearful woman came to me not long ago. She said she had been born again but had lost the joy of her salvation and lived in fear of dying. "What is wrong with my Christian life?" she asked me. Through patient questioning, I found that she read her Bible, did not participate in worldly pleasures, lived a life that should have brought comfort and joy to her heart; but when I asked her about her prayer life I found she did not pray for others . . . did not spend time thanking God and praising Him for saving her soul and keeping her day by day. Her prayers consisted of one subject – *self*. She continually begged for forgiveness and begged for help to live right. Her self-judgment was unjust because she exaggerated every minute fault and weakness in her life. Her whole prayer life was taken up with analyzing of self, and her analysis was warped and twisted. She needed to learn first of all, that only through Jesus can she or anyone else live for God. It matters not how strong she is nor how able she is to overcome temptation, she could never satisfy God.

"Ye are of God, little children, and have overcome them: *because greater is He that is in you, than he that is in the world*'' (I John 4:4). Those who overcome the world have nothing to brag about . . . we overcome the world only BECAUSE JESUS IS GREATER THAN THE WORLD. Those who know they are *weak* should remember, ''My strength is made perfect in weakness . . .'' (II Cor. 12:9). Those who overcome the world do so only through Jesus–not through their own strength and goodness. Therefore, we need to *stop looking inward* all the time and *look to Jesus*, who is able to help us to overcome the world.

Christians should not spend all their time ''cleaning windows,'' nor in trying to decide whether or not they *are* clean; we need to sun ourselves in God's blessed light, and that light will soon show us what needs cleaning. He will give us the strength and wisdom to do a good job of it! When God says, ''If we confess our sins, He will forgive us our sins,'' we must believe Him, trust that sins ARE forgiven, and praise Him for what He has done. Then *forget self* – and pray for others. The Lord Jesus Christ is able to supply every need of the soul and life of man. To be a healthy, normal Christian we must continually keep our eyes on Him. To be always looking inward–dissecting and analyzing self–will cause any Christian to become unhealthy and *useless to the cause of Christ.* Look to JESUS, the Author and Finisher of our faith.

7. Perhaps you spend too little time reading God's Word.

There is nothing that will take the place of Bible reading in the Christian life. No amount of fellowship, Christian duties, or even church-going, will feed the soul as will private daily reading of the Word of God. Our whole Christian life revolves around the Word. We are saved through the Word (I Pet. 1:23). We have victory through the Word: ''For whatsoever is born of God *over-*

cometh the world: and this is the victory that overcometh the world—even our faith" (I John 5:4). "So then faith cometh by hearing—*and hearing by the Word of God*" (Rom. 10:17). We grow in our Christian life by feeding on the Word: "As newborn babes, desire the sincere milk of the Word, *that ye may grow thereby*" (I Pet. 2:2).

If you have been neglecting to read God's Word as you should, you may rest assured that such neglect will cause you to fall short of the normal Christian life. If you have reached a place where Bible reading has become irksome and you have no healthy appetite for the Word, *force yourself to read anyway*! Do this as a duty – and as you continue, a desire will be born in your heart and you will soon have a natural craving for the Word of God that nothing else on earth will satisfy. John 15:3 says, "Now ye are clean through the Word . . . ." Even though you force yourself to daily reading of the Word, the power of the living Word does its work upon the soul. More Christians than we can count are suffering from lack of prayer and Bible reading. A revival of systematic private Bible study is much to be desired. There is no short and easy way of living a victorious, happy Christian life which can dispense with Bible study. When once you learn that lesson thoroughly, you will not have to ask the question, "What is wrong in my Christian life?"

Now may I impress upon you a solemn fact? Dedicated children of God do not with one leap go from a consecrated useful life to a defeated and unhappy one. This defeat is usually the result of months of drifting—a process so slow one is unaware of it until suddenly he asks the question, "*What is wrong*?" Therefore, I give a few "don'ts" which I hope will be a warning to drifting Christians:

1. Do not drift into a careless way of keeping Sunday.

Do not miss going to church—whether you are at home or away from home. If you miss *two consecutive Sundays* of church attendance, you will find it is easier thereafter to miss . . . and harder to make an effort to go. No doubt Satan will suggest many reasons why it would be all right for you to miss Sunday school and church, and why you should participate in "harmless" Sunday pleasures. No church-goer stops going to church all at once and starts doing things on Sunday that he would formerly have refused to do. No, he drifts gradually into doing those things. If you drift into a loose way of keeping Sunday, the Lord's Day, you will eventually lose your joy and peace in the Lord.

2. Do not drift into careless companionships.

To have fellowship and daily communion with loose-living people will definitely hinder your spiritual progress. In most cases, when a Christian drifts into association with loose companions, it is the Christian who compromises his stand for Christ and loses his testimony. If you do not rebuke your companions when they use curse words, when their habits are un-Christian, you soon think nothing of their language or their actions. You drift along with the current until your conscience is seared, and one of these days you will wake up with the realization that you are in a backslidden condition and have lost all of your joy and peace of soul. You MUST either win these friends for Christ or sacrifice your own testimony!

3. Do not drift into omitting daily Bible reading and prayer.

A Christian must watch this very carefully. One morning everything may go wrong . . . the devil may whisper, "Why take time to read the Bible or pray? Skip it this morning!" You may listen to him—and skip your daily devotions. Perhaps you intend having your Bible reading and prayer at night . . . but at the close of a busy day you forget it – or you are too tired. Another busy morning you may skip your Bible reading again – and gradually you will drift into a habit of omitting it more times than you read it!

Christians, DO NOT DRIFT INTO A BACKSLIDDEN POSITION. You may tell me you have already started to drift, and you cannot resist the strong current on which you are already launched – but *it is not too late.* Send up a cry of distress to the Lord Jesus Christ, asking Him to take command of your boat. He is stronger than the mightiest current. He will rescue you.

Ask Him to fully possess your soul, making you pure and sweet and strong. Follow in His footsteps of self-sacrifice for the sake of others. Go to no place where you would be ashamed to take Him with you. Let His friends be your friends, and see that *your* friends are *His* friends. Ask Him to put you in that position where you can please and glorify Him best.

Remember that sincere prayer and patient waiting upon God will untie the hardest knots and unravel the greatest difficulties. May God help you to find the answer to the questions in your spiritual life, and to look to our blessed Saviour for the victory, peace, and joy your heart desires.

FEARS THAT ROB OF VICTORY

FEARS THAT ROB OF VICTORY

There have been many people who have come to me earnestly seeking help from fear. My heart goes out to these people, because I know that at times they are cast into the depths of despair. The Bible says, "Fear hath torment," and surely those who *do* fear can testify to the truth of this Scripture. These people need special help, and I realize that I very definitely need the wisdom that only God can give, to direct my words as I give out the promises of comfort from the Saviour.

Since it is impossible for me to see into the hearts of those who desire deliverance from fear, I do not know whether they are truly saved or not. There are some people who *need* to fear, because they have made a false profession; they have tried to cover up their sins by pious duties. There are others who have been truly born again but the devil is disturbing their peace and causing them to have doubts and fears. Therefore it demands much wisdom on the part of a pastor or Christian worker to discourage the false hopes of some and yet, on the other hand, to encourage the timid, weak Christians. Many times when a preacher warns against false professions and vain confidences, it tends to upset and disturb young Christians. Still, there are such a great number of church members who are LOST and are deceiving themselves, it is the pastor's *duty* to warn and disturb them if he can – but as soon as he preaches against false professions, many of the weak Christians apply the message to themselves and become so disturbed and upset that the family doctor wants to send them to a psychiatrist.

In trying to help those who are truly saved and yet are disturbed by their enemy, the devil, in the form of fear, I intend to use some of the arguments that many give as the cause of the disturbance of their peace.

I.

The most frequent excuse is, "I never had any great religious experience or feeling like some have had—and this being true, could I really be saved?" This misunderstanding of salvation is often the fault of older Christians for, instead of magnifying Jesus in their testimony, they magnify their own *feelings.* Instead of testifying how to be saved "by the Word," they tell how one will *feel* when he is saved. Therefore many sinners, instead of looking to Jesus for salvation, are concentrating on a "feeling" they think they are to receive; they are not expecting Jesus in the Person of the Holy Spirit to come into their hearts, but they are expecting an emotional feeling to come over them. It is when Christians get their eyes on *feelings* that they begin to wonder if they are truly saved—because, they say, "I have never felt like other Christians."

All are saved alike—but all do not have precisely the same feelings nor the same emotional demonstrations. Outward actions depend largely on your natural make-up—and some people are of the nature to be effervescent and demonstrative, while others are more cold and reserved. Both are saved alike, both have the peace of God, both may feel alike inside—but outwardly they do not act the same. What folly then to distress yourself because you do not feel as you *think* others feel. If your experience of salvation corresponds with the Word of God, it need not distress you if you have never heard of another case just like yours.

When the children of Israel were down in Egypt and

were not allowed by Pharaoh to leave, God sent many plagues to make him change his mind. The last one was the sending of the death angel over the land. God said, "I will pass through the land of Egypt this night, and will smite all the firstborn in the land of Egypt. . . And the blood shall be to you for a token upon the houses where ye are: and when I see the blood, I will pass over you, and the plague shall not be upon you to destroy you, when I smite the land of Egypt" (Exodus 12:12,13).

The children of Israel were to put the blood on the lintel and the two side posts of the door for protection. Those who were in the house under the blood were safe; those who were not, were not safe. I doubt very seriously if every Israelite had the same kind of feeling that night. Maybe some were nervous . . . some a trifle scared, knowing the death angel was passing over—while others were perfectly calm. But it did not matter *how* they felt . . . they were SAFE as long as they were behind the blood—and it was not their *feelings* that counted on that terrible night, but *whether or not the BLOOD was applied* to the door.

The kind of feeling you have is not the important thing, but whether, according to the Word of God, you have accepted Christ. If your experience corresponds with the following Scriptures, you can know you are saved in *spite* of your feelings: John 1:12,13; Romans 10:9,13; Ephesians 2:8—"For by grace are ye saved through faith; and that not of yourselves: it is the gift of God"; and I Peter 1:23—"Being born again, not of corruptible seed, but of incorruptible, BY THE WORD OF GOD"—*not by feelings.*

II.

Many young people and many new-born babes in Christ

become very discouraged when they first realize they are not living a life of perfection. Some of them lose their temper and say or do things of which they are mortally ashamed. The moment they realize how they have acted and how they have yielded to the devil, they yield still further by listening to the devil's taunts and jeers that, "You are not saved–just look what you have done"–instead of going on their knees and claiming the promises of I John 1:9: "If we confess our sins, He is faithful and just to forgive us our sins, and to cleanse us from all unrighteousness" and I John 2:1: "My little children, these things write I unto you, that ye sin not. And if any man sin, we have an advocate with the Father, Jesus Christ the righteous."

Instead of confessing and believing the promises of the Word, they fear and say to themselves, "If I were truly a child of God, I would not fall into temptation as I do." These distressed ones do not understand the Scripture nor their position in Christ–for as long as they live in a body of flesh they will not be free from the devil's temptations, nor will they be able to live a perfect life. I know some people believe in "sinless perfection," but they are fooling themselves. Now, please do not become excited and throw down the book. I do not believe that God *winks* at sin (as some people think the Baptists believe and teach); neither do I think God gives His children license to sin a little every day. No! God deals with known presumptuous sins in the life of His child. The desire of every truly born-again child of God should be to live a clean life, free from sin – but that is a vast difference from living a perfect life. Only *One* lived a perfect life on this earth–and that was the Lord Jesus Christ.

Several places in the Scriptures we are told to live

"blameless" lives, which means "above reproach" in the eyes of the world . . . but "blameless" is far different from *perfection.* Read I Thessalonians 5:23 and I Corinthians 1:8. Another Scripture, I John 2:28, tells us, "And now, little children, abide in Him; that, when He shall appear, we may have confidence, and not be ASHAMED before Him at His coming." Also read Paul's experience in the last part of the seventh chapter of Romans, where he tells of the strife of the two natures within him–the divine nature of God warring against the fleshly nature. The question is, "Are you, as Paul, WARRING AGAINST SIN? Is it your desire to live blameless and above reproach? Do you sincerely strive to overcome the tempter and day by day live as close to God as you possibly can?" If so, do not let the enemy bother and discourage you, but put on the whole armour of God and continue to war against sin.

"From the heart come the issues of life"; God looks on the *heart,* while *man* looks on the outward appearance. Our Saviour knows the weaknesses and the frailties of the flesh–but this does not mean that God winks at sin, nor does it mean that one of His children will get by with sin. The man who has the idea that he can live a haphazard life and says, "Regardless of what I do I will not be lost" is laboring under false presumption and has never been saved–or if he *has* been saved, he is in for an awful surprise. Personally, I have my doubts about a person who has such an attitude *being* saved, because the Bible teaches that ". . . the grace of God that bringeth salvation hath appeared to all men, teaching us that, denying ungodliness and worldly lusts, *we should live soberly, righteously, and godly, in this present world*" (Tit. 2:11,12).

It is the same grace that saves us, that *teaches* us

to live a righteous life; therefore, I firmly believe that every true child of God wants to please his Saviour. Some are weaker than others, and some accomplish a closer walk with the Saviour than others–but all born-again ones are taught by the grace of God to deny ungodliness, and all *saved* people desire to please their Saviour. This change of heart and change of desire comes about with the new birth – and *without* this change, I say there has been no new birth. (Read II Corinthians 5:17.)

Take an inward look, you who fear because at times you have come short of your ideal Christian life, and see if your desire is to live a clean, consecrated life. Do not fret because you cannot live perfectly, but instead determine by God's grace and help to live blamelessly. *As long as you have a determination to war against sin, you have no need to fear.* Far too many church members are not disturbed at all about the sin in their life – so possibly, then, it is a good sign that you *have* been born again if you are disturbed about your failures in your Christian life. In answer to this, someone may be ready to say, "Instead of growing better and farther away from temptations, it seems the devil bothers me more now than when I first professed Christ as Saviour. If I were really saved, wouldn't I be getting better and less a target of the devil?" To these I reply, "To perceive more readily the temptations brought about by the devil does not prove you are not as close to God, but the reverse." The cleaner and whiter a garment, the more readily we can detect a spot of dirt just put on it, but a very dirty garment can receive many fresh spots of dirt without being noticed.

We do not know the potential excess of sin that is wrapped up in these bodies of flesh until we begin to live for God and to oppose the devil. For example, a deep river with a strong current flows peacefully along, and we do not realize the swiftness and strength of the underflow unless we try to buck the current and go up the river, or until we try to change its course. In the same manner, a person can live carelessly and without much consciousness of the power of evil passions, until he has been saved and begins a new life in Christ; then he realizes the weakness of the flesh as never before—and the longer he lives for God and the closer he gets to God, the clearer perception he has of sin and evil. This is called "growing in grace." I am sure there are very few Christians who do not continue to do some things after they are saved that later on in the Christian life they let drop—because as a Christian reads the Word, he is enlightened on certain subjects and is, by the Word, convicted of certain habits; therefore, an older Christian sees the wrong in many things that a babe in Christ does not see. It is this very thing (the ability to recognize evil more readily) that causes some people to think they are being tempted more now than when they were first saved.

We must also keep in mind that after a person is saved, the devil begins an all-out campaign to rob that one of his testimony, joy, and influence. Never think for one moment that when a person is saved, the devil folds up his tents and marches away a vanquished foe. No indeed! Instead, he starts a war right there. It is at the new birth that a man begins, as did the Apostle Paul, to "war against sin in the flesh." That is the reason I have often said there is no room in the ranks of God for "sissies." It takes *backbone* to stand up and fight the devil as a good soldier of God. However, we have no reason to fear; our Captain is victorious—and even though we come through the battle a little bloody and bruised, thank God we know we will come through victorious. Lift up your heads, you who fear . . . if you know you have been born again, do not be discouraged because the devil is fighting you as never before; that does not give you reason to doubt your salvation. Instead of moping around filled with fear and doubting, stand erect, pick up your banner and your sword, and march forward for Jesus. "Blessed is the man that endureth temptation: for when he is tried, he shall receive the crown of life, which the Lord hath promised to them that love Him" (James 1:12).

III.

I am reminded now of others who live in peace for a while and then suddenly lunge to the depths of despair because they say there is a danger of "self-deception." They argue that it is possible to join the church, be baptized, and to think you are all right but be *all wrong*. To this I say, "Indeed it *is* possible—and not only *possible*, but oftentimes *true*." I can sympathize with this kind of fear, perhaps more than with any of the others, because of a past experience in my life. Soon after I was saved, I was in a service where a man whom I had known for years and whom I believed was saved, went to the altar. When he testified, he said that although he had been in the church and done church work and had professed Christ for years, he had never been born again until that night. Immediately the devil whispered to me, "If that man was deceived, you might be also." This was the only time I have ever doubted my salvation for, I thought, surely if he could be fooled, I could too; but after becoming an older Christian, I realized that that fellow was contented to be self-deceived. He was in the church to cover up a sinful, dirty life. He was not in ignorance, as he later explained to me . . . actually he was not even deceived; he was a hypocrite. But you see how the devil used him to cause me to fear.

You who have recognized the one way of salvation, who know and believe one must be born again to go to heaven, need have no fear of being self-deceived. You admit by such testimony of fear that you have been *undeceived.* The poor group in the church who are deceived think they can get to heaven by joining the church and doing the best they can—and they are not disturbed at all because they *are deceived.* They are just as much in darkness and just as deceived as those in false religions who worship idols rather than the Saviour.

Fear is usually the best remedy against the thing feared. I feel there are none farther from the danger of making a false profession than those who are *afraid* of it. The self-deceived are generally bold and confident and are content to settle down to a false security; but you who fear self-deceit, you who fear lest you make a mistake—this is not *your* character at all. You admit that, above all things, you are anxious to be born again and on the right way to heaven—and this very fact proves that you are not the careless self-deceiver. You are not like the dishonest man who is unwilling to have his bad coin examined because he intends to pass it; you are very anxious that your profession be examined from every point to see if you are really saved or merely deceiving yourself. This one thing I can say of a surety . . . *one thing you are NOT* . . . and that is a *self-deceiver.* But why then do you live in fear and worry over self-deception? Trust God completely for your salvation and rest assured in Him – for those of you who are doubting and fearful are not in reality doubting *yourself* . . . you are doubting *God.* It is *God* who promised He would save; therefore, when you come to God and ask Him to save you, your salvation depends on GOD'S FAITHFULNESS *to keep His promise.* GOD IS FAITHFUL, and we must believe Him.

Our salvation does not rest on our faithfulness or on our works. After we are saved, *our joy and our reward* depend upon *our faithfulness.* Therefore, I ask you to trust God for your salvation; settle it now! If you have been of this fearful nature, afraid of self-deception, just get on your knees now and, in your own heart, pray the essence of this prayer: "Lord, the devil keeps bothering me by telling me that I am not saved and that I am just one of those who has deceived himself. Now, if I have never been saved, I will accept Jesus right now as my Saviour . . . please save me now." God said in His Word, "But as many as received Him, to them gave He power to become the sons of God . . . ." Did you mean it when you asked God to save you, and did you mean it when you said you would accept Him as your Saviour?

Some have said to me, "How do I know I mean it?" I try not to become impatient with these, but all I can answer is that it is a matter of intelligence. You are in your right mind and have sense enough to know if you want to be saved. However, for the benefit of some who are truly disturbed and afraid they do not know their own mind, I will say this: "As far as you can know, and the *best* you can know, you meant it when you asked Jesus to come into your heart." And to this you can answer, "Yes." Well, I want to declare unto you that *God* meant it when He said He would save you – and *God cannot lie.* His Word declares you to be His child (John 1:12,13). The Word of God says you *are saved . . .* the *devil* whispers, "Are you sure?" Whom will you believe, God or the devil? "*Abraham believed God,* and it was counted unto him for righteousness" (Rom. 4:3). Put YOUR name there . . .

say, "I BELIEVE GOD . . . God said if I would call, He would save, and if I would accept Jesus as my Saviour, I would be born into His family and would become His child. I have done this; therefore, I can *know* I am saved because *God said He would save me* . . . and I believe God."

IV.

Some have doubts and fears because they think they come far short of being what they have observed in other Christians. All that I need to reply to these people is that the worst part of those other Christians may not be known to us, or they may not have your hindrances in the Christian life. Besides, it should be taken into consideration the length of time these others have been saved. They may be mature Christians, while you, the discouraged, are still a babe in Christ. We do not grow INTO salvation; but after we are born again, we *grow in grace.* Certainly a new-born babe in Christ cannot expect to act as an older Christian or have the knowledge possessed by one who has been saved for years. My advice to you who are discouraged because you feel you are not as "good" a Christian as others, is to put your eyes on *Jesus* instead of your fellow-Christian. Just be thankful that there *are* some Christians you know whom you believe do live close to God.

On the other hand, do not get your eyes on *people* because, even though you have great confidence in someone now, he *could* disappoint you later. Whereas, if you keep your eyes on the LORD, *He* will *never* disappoint you nor let you down – and if you will learn this lesson early in your Christian life, it will save you from disappointment. Just remember, no Christian is perfect, regardless of how exalted he is in your mind–and neither is he infallible. Therefore, with this knowledge firmly impressed upon your mind, you can rejoice with any Christian who is living as you think a Christian should, and you will not be thrown into the depths of despair should the "exalted" one fall. Keep your heart and eyes turned to Jesus, not your fellowman.

V.

Now, another class of people (and these are becoming more numerous) say they fear that they have not been saved because such evil thoughts come into their mind. Here again one has to be so careful, for I do not wish to give these people false hope, and I certainly do not want to mislead these fearful ones in the least.

When dealing face to face with these people, I question them at length as to whether they have ever been saved–and if they have doubts, then we deal first with the salvation question; but even then, this question will pop up again: "Why do I have these thoughts?"

We are told that everything we read and learn makes a tiny groove in our brain. The knowledge is there. We think we have forgotten, but later these thoughts will come back to us. While a sinner, many of these people have read lewd magazines and participated in ungodly pleasures, and years later–even after they are saved–the devil brings these thoughts back to the mind. This is a very big reason why young people should be very careful what they read and to what they listen, because it does not "go in one ear and out the other"–but instead, it makes a lasting impression on the mind, and years later the ghost of memory can come back to torment them.

I have had people tell me that they have had thoughts that had never entered their mind before–something they have never read about, something they have never had a part in–and this only proves to me that there is a supernatural enemy at work. It is the *devil's* work, and he is powerful enough . . . real enough . . . to put these thoughts at the door of your mind, or to actually whisper them to your mind—and therefore, it is not you at all, it is not your thoughts, but the *devil's.* You who are saved will have to admit that these thoughts do not come from the heart and that they are an evil you hate and thoughts you want to be rid of.

The devil can whisper to the mind, but he cannot tamper with the *heart*—for God's seal is upon the heart of His children (Eph. 4:30). It is not sinful for the devil to whisper thoughts to you, but it *is* sinful if you allow them to possess your mind and to become *your* thoughts. If these evil thoughts *do not disturb you* and you continue to entertain such thoughts, finally possessing them as your own, I feel you have need to fear that you are not saved. *Saved* people do not want to entertain evil thoughts, and it becomes a cause of great distress when they are bothered by the devil with them.

I realize this is a very elusive temptation to fight. If it were tangible—something we could see and fight openly—it would be much easier, but thoughts slip in unaware any time, any place. Do not become discouraged, my Christian friend; *there is victory in Jesus.* If you really *want* to be rid of terrible thoughts, your duty is to call upon Jesus to banish the "disturber." You are no match for the devil—and if you try to argue with him concerning your thoughts, or ponder them in your mind, the devil will be the victor. Michael, the archangel, did not argue with the devil over the body of Moses, but said, "The *Lord* rebuke thee" (Jude 9).

The split second an evil thought pops into your mind, call on Jesus to drive it away—and if it persists, start singing or go out doors for a good, stiff walk. Outdoor exercise is especially good for young people who are tormented with the devil's thoughts. Read God's Word daily—and even though you do not understand the Word, its cleansing power will clear your mind: "Now ye are clean through the Word" (John 15:3). Then, cultivate good thoughts. "Finally, brethren, whatsoever things are true, whatsoever things are honest, whatsoever things are just, whatsoever things are pure, whatsoever things are lovely, whatsoever things are of good report; if there be any virtue, and if there be any praise, *think on these things*" (Phil. 4:8).

My friend, to make an acid test regarding the evil thoughts that come into your mind, determine whether these thoughts grieve you or not. If you do not delight in them, but instead you strive against them . . . then they are no evidence against your salvation. Your great defense now is to recognize the devil's work and to call upon your Saviour to banish evil thoughts and to keep your mind clean. As I have already said, "Your part then is to read the Word, pray, resist, and think on pure things."

VI.

Sometimes fears and doubts are caused by physical weakness. How often I have seen precious women stormed by doubts and fears when they are going through a time of nervous disorder. When their body and mind are weakened by sickness, then the devil tries his best to disturb them and cause them to doubt and fear. If these people would realize that their trouble is *physical* instead of *spiritual*, then they would win the victory. If they would stop listening to the devil and in full confidence trust the Lord to see them through, then as their nervous system is strengthened and their body is healed, the doubts would go—and they would wonder why they ever had such fears.

Therefore I say to you, my Christian friend, "If you are physically ill, do not allow the devil to make you doubt God." Trust God completely, and when you come through this sickness, you will be as gold tried in fire. "Wherefore let them that suffer according to the will of God commit the keeping of their souls to Him in well doing, as unto a faithful Creator" (I Peter 4:19).

VII.

Finally, there is a group of people who fear they are not saved because they are afraid of death. I realize that death is an unwelcome visitor; the Bible calls death an *enemy*: "The last enemy that shall be destroyed is death" (I Cor. 15:26). Here again we must be very careful not to give false hope. I tremble as I try to give help to these fearful ones, but it is a shame for God's child to go on in fear in regard to death.

It is only natural for a person to dread going through the door of death; we all have a tendency to dread some new ordeal through which we have to pass, and such a tendency only goes with a body of flesh. God's Word, though, gives comfort to the born again–if they will only believe and trust the future to God: "O death, where is thy sting? O grave, where is thy victory? The sting of death is sin . . ." (I Cor. 15:55,56). Please notice that *death* is not the sting, but that the sting of death is *sin.* Jesus came to take away the sin of the world (John 1:29), and for those who are saved, *the sting of death is removed.*

In the twenty-third Psalm, God's Word gives us comfort if we would only accept it literally. The Psalmist says, "Yea, though I walk THROUGH the valley of the shadow of death, *I will fear no evil: for THOU art with me*; thy rod and thy staff they comfort me." First, notice the word "THROUGH." Thank God, we are not going *into* the valley and wander around . . . we are going *through.* The victory is already certain; we have the assurance that we will not have to linger or stay in the valley of death, but we are going through it. Our Saviour has already conquered death for us, and we need have no fear. "Forasmuch then as the children are partakers of flesh and blood, He also Himself likewise took part of the same; that through death He might destroy him that had the power of death, that is, the devil; and deliver them who through fear of death were all their lifetime subject to bondage" (Heb. 2:14,15). Jesus Himself said, "I am He that liveth, and was dead; and, behold, I am alive for evermore, Amen; and have the keys of hell and of death" (Rev. 1:18).

One thing is assured, my Christian friend: we are all going through that valley and out on the other side – but notice next the word "SHADOW." We are only going through the *shadow* of death. Most people speak of the valley of death as a terribly dark passage, but for the Christian, it is not. To have a shadow there must be *light,* because in perfect darkness there can be no shadow. There has to be some light to produce a shadow – and the light in that valley of death, as we go through, is *Jesus Christ, the Light of the world.* Jesus has promised to go with us all the way, even through the valley of the shadow of death. Even if the enemy, death, should claim these bodies, the Lord will go with us to comfort us. This is where we must trust Him. As you look toward death now, it may look terrible; but it is up to you as a child of God to trust the Lord to keep His Word and to give you comfort and dying grace when the time comes. You do not need dying grace now – you need grace to *live* for Him.

Dying Grace
(Psalm 23:4)

Since death is but the opening of a door
Into a larger, fairer room . . . nay, more
It is the welcoming of His voice, the touch
Of His dear hand on ours at last . . . if such
Is death, why should we ever be afraid
Or doubt that He will keep the promise made?
Then trust Him, frightened child, for He will give
Us grace to die who gives us grace to live!
Await His time . . . do we need dying grace
While we are living? But when, face to face
With that last moment, He will take our hand
To lead us home, and we shall understand
And smile at fear, and smiling, enter, for
Our death will be the opening of His door!

It would be an endless task to list all the ways in which doubts and fears assail us; those I have mentioned are only a few, but regardless of what they are, they can be cast out by the Lord Jesus Christ. Many seem to think that they show a commendable spirit by cherishing such fears, as if it were an evidence of their humility and a sense of unworthiness—but there is no humility in doubting God's promises. I John 4:18 says, ". . . He that feareth is not made perfect in love." In the Amplified New Testament, the meaning is made clearer: "There is no fear in love . . . dread does not exist; but full-grown (complete, perfect) love turns fear out-of-doors and expels every trace of terror! For fear brings with it the thought of punishment and (so) he who is afraid has not reached the full maturity of love . . . is not yet grown into love's complete perfection." Those of you who fear dying do not completely trust your Saviour to see you through; you have not completely trusted Him in this matter, fully knowing that all will be well because He will be with you.

I know that some of God's children have been ignorant of His promises, and this ignorance has caused them to fear – but now you know, and it is unworthy of you to doubt and to fear death when God has so graciously promised His presence and comfort to you through the valley of the shadow of death. The same thing holds true in any other fear you may have–for when you completely trust the Lord and your love is full-grown, you will rest assured in the Lord, knowing that He doeth all things well.

"Be careful for nothing; but in every thing by prayer and supplication with thanksgiving let your requests be made known unto God. And the peace of God, which passeth all understanding, shall keep your hearts and minds through Christ Jesus" (Phil. 4:6,7).

"STAND YE STILL . . . FEAR NOT, NOR BE DISMAYED"

"STAND YE STILL... FEAR NOT, NOR BE DISMAYED"

"And David said in his heart, I shall now perish one day by the hand of Saul: there is nothing better for me than that I should speedily escape into the land of the Philistines" (I Sam. 27:1).

We have here the feelings and decision of a very discouraged man. In the preceding chapters, we find that David had many times escaped death from the hand of King Saul. It is true that he had been driven from place to place by the king, and many attempts had been made on his life—but God had always protected him. In spite of this, we find him here discouraged, without hope, and thinking there is no security for him in Judea. This is the man who has slain his giant and with God's protection escaped death; but in a moment of discouragement, he seems to have forgotten all the victories of the past and makes a rash resolve to go among the Philistines.

We wonder why David could ever think that he would die by the hand of Saul after he had been anointed by Samuel and had received God's promise that the kingdom would be *his.* When he knew that he was to succeed Saul to the throne, how could he ever entertain the thought that he would die before God was ready for him to sit upon that throne? In absolute faith he stood before the giant and said, "This day will the Lord deliver thee into mine hand." So it is with us: we stand the test well under the large trials, we with courage go forth to slay our giants—but we fret and chafe under the constant annoyance of a little mosquito. David had become irritated, disturbed, and discouraged under the constant strain of running from Saul, and finally he gave up in defeat, saying, "There is nothing better for me than that I should speedily escape into the land of the Philistines."

By going into the enemy's territory, David was led into many evils that would not have touched him had he remained in Israel. For one thing, he had to live a lie. He gave the King of Gath false impressions of his loyalty to the cause of the Philistines by pretending that he was going to fight against the Israelites, when he had no intention of fighting against his own people. This, of necessity, put him in a very awkward position—for there he was in the enemy's territory seeking protection, and yet his heart and soul were for his own nation. He was on the wrong side of the fence, and this involved him still deeper in treachery. When he went out conquering, he had to resort to cruelty because he had to slay all men, women, and children so that not one could escape to tell the King of Gath what had been done. Once during the absence of David and his men, the Amalekites invaded his city and carried off all the women and children; because of this, David's life was threatened by his own men in their grief over their terrible loss.

I hardly see how David could have suffered more dangers, even if he had remained in Judea under Saul's persecutions, than he suffered while in the enemy's territory. I am sure of one thing: he would not have been guilty of so many sins had he remained in Judea. To be sure, he would have been driven from place to place—but his life would have been secure because he would have been protected by God. And most important, he would have been among his own countrymen in the land where people believed in God. I believe David would have been just as secure in Israel as in Gath – and what David suffered there was brought about by a hasty resolve made in a moment of discouragement.

This incident in David's life is worth our attention so that we might profit thereby, for it shows us that we are not to try to remove life's barriers by resorting to unlawful means–and especially is it wrong to resort to these means in moments of discouragement. It may further teach us that under all circumstances, *the path of DUTY is the path of SAFETY*. In II Chronicles 20:17 we find the following instruction and promise to God's people: *"Ye shall not need to fight in this battle: set yourselves, STAND YE STILL, and see the salvation of the Lord with you, O Judah and Jerusalem: FEAR NOT, NOR BE DISMAYED; . . . for the Lord will be with you."*

Under pressure of trials, we naturally seek relief; but if an upright, legitimate way is not present, then we are tempted to use the wrong means. Under stress, we argue with ourselves that the way we are taking is right; yet under other circumstances we would condemn others for doing this very thing. Many times a Christian feels led of the Lord to undertake a certain course; yet because of obstacles in the way, he turns aside to take an easier path and one he thinks will have fewer difficulties. But I wonder if compromise is the easier path after all. Like David, he will meet Philistines . . . like Jonah, who shunned preaching to Nineveh, he encounters the storm and the whale.

Most of the time, Christians who make hasty decisions while under trials and discouragement, later repent their decision. A person who is discouraged, depressed, and under pressure is not always able to make a right decision, because the mind is bound to be clouded by the sorrow of the heart. Many people, under stress, resort to suicide – and I am sure many of these suicides would not occur if those discouraged ones would only wait a while longer before making such a tragic decision. Extreme depression borders on insanity, hence many of the foolish and tragic acts performed by depressed people.

Christians are not exempt from becoming discouraged, for the devil has made it his business to hinder and worry God's children; but God will bring His children out of the "slough of despondency" if they will only trust Him and be patient. However, there is great danger and possibility of making a wrong turn during this time of discouragement.

God's preachers, of all people, should know the devil's subtle tricks; but although they should *know* better, there are many of them who, during a time of struggle, have sacrificed principles. I have heard of preachers who have become discouraged in their present pastorate, deciding that the only thing to do was to get into the "machine" so they would be backed by the "big shots" and not have to worry or have so much opposition. They took what they thought the easier road. They did the very thing that they had preached against months before. Even though they gained a larger church and preached to more people, they did wrong to sacrifice their convictions and to compromise with organized religion.

How often I have heard Dr. Bob Jones, Sr. say, "*It is never right to do wrong in order to get a chance to do right.*" It is not right to sell out to be able to preach to larger crowds; it is not the safer way and it is not the *best* way. It amazes me that some of God's preachers will not trust Him to secure them a place to preach, depending, instead, on the "brethren." They say, "If I get in with the fellows of this convention, I am assured of a place to preach." How small do they think their God is? Instead of putting their faith in a BIG GOD to protect them against their "Sauls" in seasons of discouragement, they turn to *men* for help.

There are *wives* who for years stand true to God and do not compromise their belief to please an ungodly husband–yet in a time of utter discouragement they say, "What is the use of fighting against him longer," and they give in and follow him into something that they know is wrong. Such a decision is bound to result in heartache and regret. Could they only stop and think back to the times God has given them grace and strength to withstand the wiles of the devil wielded through their husband, they would surely say, "I will yet stand true, though it kills me." Wives whose affections are trampled on and whose very hearts are well-nigh broken, are easy prey to discouragement. But just remember, that is no time to make a momentous decision or to give way to temptation. ". . . God is faithful, who will not suffer you to be tempted above that ye are able; but will with the temptation also make a way to escape, that ye may be able to bear it" (I Cor. 10:13).

Young people who live a separated life sometimes become lonely, and loneliness often leads to discouragement. The devil whispers, "Is the Christian life worth it?" To those who yield to the tempter I say, "Beware!" Compromising with the world to enjoy greater popularity is a terrible mistake; and such a rash decision does not lead to peace and joy, but to unhappiness and remorse. After the cloud of despondency lifts–and it does not linger long with young people–they find that the path they have chosen IS NOT WHAT THEY REALLY WANTED AFTER ALL.

There are many ways a Christian can make wrong

decisions under stress and trial; however, I will not endeavor to name any more. You know how the devil tempts you the most and in what manner you are most easily discouraged. But *God also knows* and is willing to give you aid. As the old colored preacher prayed, "Lord, prop me on my leaning side," so we need to pray and guard carefully our weak points of defense. God will help you—and you need not become discouraged as David did, if you will only remember that *He is able.* "God is our refuge and strength, a very present help in trouble" (Psa. 46:1).

We know *the devil is on the job to DISCOURAGE GOD'S CHILDREN*—and it is not so bad to have these feelings if we do not make rash decisions while we are discouraged. Oh! If you would only realize this, Christian, and remember it if you should at any time become discouraged and tempted, as David was, to seek an escape outside of God's will.

When the Christian is tempted to seek relief by the wrong method and not one of God's leading, he should always look back to the time when he was happy in the Lord and not under stress, and he should ask himself, "What would I have thought of such a decision *then*?" He then should follow what his heart tells him he would have done at that time, and not what his present discouraged feelings tell him to do. He must say, "I am not in a state of mind now to make a wise decision—but I know how I once felt about this thing, and I will keep to my former path."

However, if you become so mixed up in your thinking that you do not *know* what you once would have done or know what to do *now*, DO NOTHING. Just STAND STILL AND WAIT until you *do* know what to do. Regardless of how imperative you think it is to give a decision concerning some problem, you must not do so now unless you KNOW it is the right one—and when the deadline comes and you *must* decide, God will show you in some way what to do. It is far better to *stand still and wait*, than to make the wrong decision. ". . . Set yourselves, *stand ye still*, and see the salvation of the Lord . . ." (II Chron. 20:17).

As you look back on your past life, are you not glad that you did not follow all the purposes you decided upon when you were despondent and not truly yourself? God's children are so much like small boys who become incensed at being punished—and what they consider wronged by their parents—and they say, "I will run away from home, and *then* they will be sorry." But when darkness comes they are glad to be home under the protection of the parental roof rather than out on some highway by themselves; for by the time darkness has come, both the feeling of hurt and the desire to run away are gone.

I direct my remarks now to Christian workers who many times become discouraged in the visible result of their work for the Lord; they labor, toil, and pray—and yet it all seems so futile. How often we find these tired, discouraged workers saying, "I am not accomplishing anything; I might as well quit"—and then they take up some other plan with fewer opportunities to win souls but with less heartache and trials. What a sad thing for a Christian to do. When one is discouraged is not the time to abandon the field of service to the enemy. Instead, it is time to look to God's precious Word, where He tells us, "They that sow in tears shall reap in joy. He that goeth forth and weepeth, bearing precious seed, shall doubtless come again with rejoicing, bringing his sheaves with him" (Psa. 126:5,6). "*. . . Fear not, NOR BE DISMAYED . . . for the Lord will be with you.*"

Keep pressing on. THE VICTORY IS THE LORD'S, and ere long you will see the fruit of your labor; then when you are out of the bonds of despondency, you will be better able to think clearly about your work—whether to keep on where you are or to enter another field of service. If God has led you into a certain path, regardless how dark and rough it may seem now, He will lead you safely through; for He goeth before the sheep and, by faith, you will see His footprints in the sand. On the other hand, if you take another road, it may be full of difficulties that the right path does not hold.

Our subject may also be applied to another class of people: those "earnest seekers" who have made many efforts to gain the assurance of salvation and yet have failed. Sometimes these unsaved ones become discouraged and say, "There is no use for me to go to the altar or to try to be saved; I have tried so many times and failed." This is a very foolish resolve and is born only of a discouraged heart. In many instances, Christians are unsympathetic with this group and usually lay their failure to the fact that they are UNWILLING to be saved. But this is not always the case, for there are many who earnestly *desire* to be saved but who have not the hope of salvation.

Sometimes these people are hindered by ignorance concerning salvation; they are harboring beliefs of false traditions and false impressions of what the "new birth" really is. They have been taught that great emotional feeling accompanies salvation. They earnestly pray for God to save them, and then wait for something unusual to occur—even though they themselves do not know what they are waiting for. All they can say is, "When I am saved, I will know it"; and I agree with them, but not in the way they mean.

Sometime ago, I talked to a lady in the inquiry room who earnestly prayed for God to save her. Sincerely she told me she desired to be saved above all else—and I believed her. I showed her the Word, explaining the way of salvation; but after an hour of ardent prayer and explanation, she went away in doubt. I asked her what she was waiting for—and she had to admit she did not know. How heartbreaking to have to allow a poor soul to go away blinded by the devil; but how much *more* heartbreaking it must be to *Jesus*, who gave Himself for her and offers her eternal salvation as a free gift, and yet she will not accept Him. She was unable to accept Christ by faith; she had some preconceived idea of what she would do or the way she would feel when she was saved. That lady had the "cart before the horse." She prayed for God to save her—and then waited for a feeling or experience to *prove* to her that God had kept His word and had saved her. Without some physical feeling as proof, she would not believe God. She *should* have BELIEVED GOD FIRST—and then peace and joy would have entered her soul.

Some years ago, a fine man came to the altar in the tent night after night. All effort to help him proved in vain. Finally one night, my husband prevailed upon the man to tell him just what was keeping him from accepting Christ. He said he would never believe he was saved *until he shouted.* He said his grandmother "shouted all over the church" when she was saved—and he knew that if ever *he* was saved, *he* would shout also. Before the meeting closed, however, he *believed the Word* and was saved—without shouting.

In a way, this stubborn unbelief disgusts Christian workers, but it should not. Instead, it should bring a sense of pity and a burdened heart which will lead to much prayer for these deluded souls. When Christians accuse them of being hardheaded although *they* believe themselves willing to be saved, it tends to discourage them from ever "trying again."

Now, we know for a surety that God will save them in a moment, and that it is God's *will* to save. We also know that nothing but *unbelief* keeps them from salvation (John 3:18). But such a person needs instruction and encouragement instead of discouragement and reproof. God forbid that we should take away hope from any heart; for, let the sinner begin to feel it is useless to try, and he will not be long in deciding he will hold no restraints upon his life and will begin sinking deeper and deeper into sin. He will say as did the people in Jeremiah's day, "There is no hope: but we will walk after our own devices, and we will every one do the imagination of his evil heart" (Jer. 18:12).

A beggar will sometimes knock at a door until he is convinced there is no one inside to take notice of his need—and then he will curse those who live within. Just so, let the sinner become convinced that there is no hope and that God has hardened His heart against him, and then that sinner will harden *his* heart against God.

Christian, beware then of taking hope away from those who say they want to be saved and yet are still outside of Christ. It would be wise to distinguish between the willful, hardened sinner and the sincere but perplexed inquirer. If you are not sure, give him the benefit of the doubt and exercise patience and longsuffering toward that sinner.

And now I speak to the *perplexed, sincere sinner*—and I beg of YOU to *beware of yielding to discouragement* and thence to deeper sin. Have you already taken up David's resolution and said, "One day I shall perish in an everlasting hell; so there is nothing better for me to do than to cast my lot with the world . . . with the enemies of Christ"? If you have, I want to warn you it is no light thing to refuse eternal salvation and to trample underfoot the precious blood of Jesus, which was shed for you. This foolish resolve made in a moment of discouragement will not only mean heartache in this world, but an eternity in hell.

If you were in a burning building, would you cease to hunt for an outlet? No, you would seek a way out UNTIL THE VERY FLAMES ENGULFED YOU and you lost consciousness; and even then, your last thought and prayer would be that someone would find you ere it was too late. If you would be so persevering to escape a *physical* death in flames, how much more you should seek to escape an ETERNAL death in *hell.* As long as there is breath in your body, you should not cease to try to find the way of salvation; and just because you have "tried and failed" is no reason why you should not try again. Keep in mind always that *it is not God's will* for ONE to perish, but that ALL should come to repentance (II Peter 3:9).

It is not that God will not save you or that you cannot be saved, for *God is faithful* and will do just what He *promised* He would do – but you are still groping in darkness because *the devil has blinded your mind.* Please forget all former ideas of what will happen when you are saved, and trust your soul into the Saviour's hand NOW. You already realize you are bound for hell and cannot save yourself; therefore, do you not think it would be wise to trust God's Word and believe Him for salvation *because He has promised*? Abraham "staggered not at the promise of God through unbelief; but was strong in faith, giving glory to God; and being fully persuaded that, WHAT HE HAD PROMISED, HE WAS ABLE ALSO TO PERFORM" (Rom. 4:20,21).

Arise, discouraged sinner, renew thy petitions; and if a *lifetime* spent in blind inquiries ends in eternal salvation, it will be worth every moment spent. "For what is a man profited, if he shall gain the whole world, and lose his own soul?" (Matt. 16:26).

Our Scripture and warning can also be directed and applied to *backsliders.* The devil is very busy trying to keep backsliders in such a state of mind that they will not come back to God; and how often I have seen despairing backsliders in the prayer room, weeping because they had no hope. They say, "I have tried and failed; I know God will not bother with me again. There is no use to ask for forgiveness."

In the outset, let me make it perfectly clear that when I speak of backsliders, I mean those who have been *truly born again.* Thousands of church members who profess to be backsliders are *not,* in the true sense of the word, for they were never really saved in the beginning. All they did was join the church and for a while "turn over a new leaf"; but to "slide back" from God, you have to first be in true fellowship with God. Therefore, I want to impress upon your minds that all are not backsliders who *claim* to be. If there is any doubt in your mind as to whether you have ever been saved, *forget* the word "backslider," and seek God for SALVATION. If all you possess is a church letter, you do not need to be *reclaimed* . . . you need to be REBORN.

Regardless of the fact that there are scores of so-called backsliders who have never "slid up," there are many true backsliders who are living in misery, hopelessness, and despair. By God's grace, I want to show you *there are no grounds for despair.* In order to do this, I will give the main reason why some are so discouraged, and then I hope by God's Word to show them that they need not despair.

There are some people who, by their own reasoning, declare they have no hope. They put God on the same level with man and say, "It is not reasonable that God would *keep on* forgiving." They reason that even our best friends or our closest loved ones would eventually get tired of forgiving, and one could not *expect* a holy God to put up with such a "sorry person as I"; therefore, in despair and utter hopelessness they declare they *want* to come back to God and live close to Him, but are ashamed to ask again.

I am thoroughly convinced in my own heart that *any backslider* who has a *desire* to be reclaimed, to be forgiven, *CAN be* – for it is the Holy Spirit of God who convicts of sin and woos the backslider back to God. Were there no hope, God would not call. How utterly foolish it would be for God to convince, draw, and call His wayward child if He had already said about that one, "Ephraim is joined to idols: let him alone."

The *devil* has never given a sinner or a backslider the desire to come to God. A man, of his own volition, cannot draw *himself* to God, for the natural state of man has no drawing power toward God. "The natural man receiveth not the things of the Spirit of God: for they are foolishness unto him: neither can he know them, because they are spiritually discerned" (I Cor. 2:14). Therefore, we may conclude that *only GOD* calls or gives the desire for a man to come to that "fountain filled with blood" that cleanses from all sin.

My backslider friend, never forget that *God knows you by name*—and if He has called you, drawn you, convicted you, and given you the desire to return to the Father's house, rest assured that it is not too late for you to be forgiven. Even though His forgiveness toward you has exceeded the number "seventy times seven" and you have no confidence in yourself to stand, if you hear the Saviour's call, *you had better come.* Come out from behind your excuses of despair and hopelessness; your failures and doubts are easily submerged in the wonderful, sufficient grace of the Lord Jesus Christ. God knows your weakness and your miserable failures. On one occasion Jesus said that He knew what was in man; He knew the frailties, the weaknesses, and the power of the flesh and the devil. It was because of the utter helplessness of man to save himself that Jesus died. He is longsuffering, not willing that any should perish . . . *His mercy endureth forever.*

It is absolutely foolish for anyone to say that God will not forgive him because he has been so weak and has sinned over and over again. He is simply putting God on man's level—judging God by what man would do under similar circumstances. Do away with such absurd fancies; does not God's Word say, "I am God, and not man" (Hosea 11:9), and "For thy mercy is great above the heavens . . ." (Psa. 108:4)?

We cannot measure the mercy or longsuffering of God with our finite minds, but it is enough for us to simply *believe the Scripture* when God says, "If we confess our sins, He is faithful and just to forgive us our sins, and to cleanse us from all unrighteousness" (I John 1:9). No one can truly confess his sins unless first he has "godly sorrow" for his sins. I realize it is unreasonable in man's sight for God to forgive you after the way you have lived, but God does not see or reason like man.

There is no one who is so miserable as a backslider. A *sinner* can enjoy his pleasures – but a *backslider . . . never.* He is miserable at church because he knows he is not right with God; he is miserable in the *world* because God's Spirit convicts him that he is out of place.

Backslider, your burden of sin is too heavy for you to bear. Will you right now come to the "fountain filled with blood" and be cleansed? Do not despair and make foolish resolves, becoming more entangled in the devil's net; but say, as the prodigal son said, "I will arise and go to my father" – and you will find, as the prodigal did, that our *heavenly* Father will welcome you with open arms.

May God help you . . . *every discouraged soul* . . . to look to Jesus – TODAY. He will lift you up "out of the miry clay" and set your feet "upon a rock" (Psa. 40:2). "*. . . Set yourselves, stand ye still . . . fear not, nor be dismayed . . . for the Lord will be with you*" (II Chron. 20:17).

LIVING IN THE PRESENT

LIVING IN THE PRESENT

"Forgetting those things which are behind" (Philippians 3:13).

"Take therefore no thought for the morrow" (Matthew 6:34).

"Redeeming the time" (Ephesians 5:16).

We are facing perilous times! Only God knows what the next week or the next year will bring forth. Many face each day with fear and despair; others face it with indifference and unconcern. I repeat, however, that we are living in and facing tremendous and perilous times, times of uncertainty, times when there are many, many international and national problems that we cannot solve, or even *help* to solve–except through prayer. It will do us no good to worry or fret about either the things that are coming upon the world or the conditions which presently exist. We who are living in the ordinary paths of life do not have the power, influence, or position to work out national problems; therefore, as children of God, as citizens of the God-given land of America, what is our duty toward the future?

It is our duty to live EACH DAY as God would have us live, praying for the leaders of our land who are in authority. And as God gives us strength and grace, we should live *one day at a time.* None of us knows what we will have tomorrow; thus it is our solemn duty to "redeem the time," making the best of each opportunity that is presented to us.

Our duty is to live in the PRESENT–not in the *past* or in the *future.* However, there are many people who live in the past instead of the present. Often I have met people who spend hours of thought and worry grieving over their past; they are forever rebuking themselves for lost opportunities or past sins. Constantly, the cry from their soul is, "If only I had taken advantage of that opportunity." This is a great mistake, because it can do no good; rather, it does much harm, for instead of helping to relieve, it *increases* the burden. Somewhere I have read this statement, and it is so true: "The only way to get rid of the past is by getting a future out of it." And the only way to get a future out of the past is to *live in the present.* The past is fixed beyond a possibility of a change—and all our worry, all our regrets, cannot change one minute of the past. How useless, then, to worry over a past which cannot be reclaimed; how foolish to waste precious time by spending hours grieving over past deeds!

I met a lady recently who was in the pitiful condition of living in the past; her home was wrecked, and instead of trying to do something to improve the situation, she was overwhelmed with sorrow and remorse over the past. She had completely given up hope. Over and over again she would say, "It might have been otherwise," or "If I had only done so and so, it would have been different." While she was grieving over the past, she was wasting her present. I begged her to confess her past to God, let Him forgive and put every sin under the blood; then she could start out anew, utilizing the precious time in her present. Then in the future when she looked back at *THIS* time, there would be no regrets.

God puts our sins away; He forgets them (Heb. 8:12). Even though we are not capable of erasing them from our memory, we should not continually bring them to mind and grieve over them. What GOD has forgiven, we should leave alone. He said He would cast our sins "into the depths of the sea" (Micah 7:19)—and when God, in His infinite mercy and grace, forgives our sins and buries them in the depths of the sea, it is wrong for us to keep digging them up. Not only should we not dig up our *own* sins, but neither should we seek to expose those of our *fellowman*. When God forgives and saves a wretched sinner, his fellowmen should not be forever throwing up the past in his face. If a holy God can forgive and put the past under the blood, we who have not been sinned against, and we who were also sinners once, should be willing to forget a man's sinful past.

This brings to my mind an incident that happened to one of my best friends. Going to school together, we were the closest of friends; but my family moved, and we were separated for several years. When I saw her next, she had become an alcoholic. She was from a very aristocratic family—but the liquor bottle is no respecter of persons, and she was its victim. She came to our evangelistic meeting and was saved. Some weeks later, while waiting in her doctor's office, she looked over her chart. Filled with accounts of treatment for her drunken sprees, it was not a pretty record. She picked it up and said to her doctor, "Doctor, God saved me from all this a few weeks ago, and according to His Word, He has given me a new record sheet. I do not like the looks of this; would *you* give me a new one also?" Thank God for a sympathetic doctor! He said, "If God can give you a clean record, I can do no less"—and he tore up the sinful record of the past and put it in the waste basket.

A lot of church members are not willing to do this for their fellow Christians. They keep on file all the old sins of their acquaintances, and then they pull those sins of the past out every so often to thrust them in the person's face. This is wrong, and those who do this should ask God to forgive them and to help them leave the past sins of others where God has put them: "For thou hast cast all my sins *behind thy back*" (Isaiah 38:17); "As far as the east is from the west, *so far hath He removed our transgressions from us*" (Psalm 103:12).

I recently had a letter from a young wife who was greatly distressed because her husband would not let her past lie buried. They both accepted Christ after they were married; yet the husband continued to throw up his wife's past sins—things she did before she was married. Because of this, their home had become very unhappy and the wife lived in torment. She never knew when he would have a fit of jealousy, condemn and reproach her for her past. She, of course, did wrong; but she had been forgiven by God, she had asked the forgiveness of her husband, and he had said he would forgive her—but he was not willing to go on from there, "forgetting those things which are behind," and live unto the present.

There is another group who live in the past. These people spend their time glorying in what they, or their ancestors, have done. They sit in a state of self-satisfaction, saying, "Look what I have done," and thus they allow precious opportunities to slip by. They are satisfied with what they have accomplished, and by their actions say, "I have done as much as or *more* than most people; I am satisfied now to sit down and rest; I do not need to do anything more." They act as if there were no souls to be saved, nothing more to do. How foolishly and sinfully they act! The fact that we have done well in the past will not, and *cannot*, exempt us from working in the present. It would be like the man who said, "I have tithed my weekly income for twenty years, and I think that is sufficient. For the *next* twenty, I will give nothing; I will appropriate all to my own personal use."

The past stands on its own merits; the present must answer for itself—and remember this: TODAY'S PRESENT will be TOMORROW'S PAST. If you want a good past with no regrets, you must make a good record *today*—and whatever we may have accomplished in the past, it does not answer for NOW. *God holds us responsible for the PRESENT*! Thus we see that good deeds done in the past do not suffice for the present, and we have no excuse to neglect the duties of the present because of our past conduct, whether it was good or bad. It is our duty to *leave the past* in the hands of the Lord, where it is and where it belongs.

There is still another group who draw comparisons between the past and the present, to the detriment of the present. They say, "The former days were better than these, the world is going to the bad, everything is on the downward trend." So instead of trying to make the present *better*, they fold their arms and bow down as worshippers of the past. They say, "No use trying to have a revival, this is the end time, we are living in the apostasy . . . there is a great 'falling away,' and there is nothing we can do about it." Then they do all they can to make their doctrine true. Yes, they do *absolutely nothing*, and they are content to accept this excuse for the failure of sinners to come to the house of God. Whereas, if every church member would get out and work *twice as hard* because there IS a falling away, the church would be filled. *It can be done*—because there are churches that are *doing* it! Not only do they work during revival time, but EVERY WEEK they put forth an effort to get people to come to church. Granting that it was easier to get sinners to church in the past, *that is no excuse* for anyone to sit down and do nothing; on the contrary, it should be an incentive to work *harder* and do a little *more* than we did in the past.

We should try to *improve* upon the past, but this can be done only by *living in the present,* only by seizing every opportunity that crosses our path. Those who live in this way will have no time to waste with their pessimistic philosophy on a great past and a terrible present. I admit that the devil is in an all-out campaign to damn souls, but this gives us no excuse to relax and take it easy. It is true that in the last days, "Evil men and seducers shall wax worse and worse, deceiving, and being deceived" (II Tim. 3:13) – but this should cause Christians to wage a fiercer battle, to be more diligent in the Lord's work. If it took just one telephone call twenty years ago to get a sinner to come to church, then today we should be willing to make *twenty* calls, if necessary, and use every legitimate means to compel them to come to Christ. As it becomes more difficult to win souls, Christians should put forth more effort and work harder than ever before.

In one sense, it is RIGHT to live in the past. By this I mean it is right to use the past as a *stepping stone* to a *better present.* The mistakes and the accomplishments of the past come to us as a sacred trust; in this we have a decided advantage over those who lived before us, because we can profit by their mistakes and by their victories. Therefore, this age could be *better* than the past, and we should make a constant effort to make it so.

However, let us not use the past to justify our "lying

down on the job'' or to excuse our half-filled churches. If we do, we aid the devil in his campaign for souls and we help to increase "the falling away.'' Please let us remember, *God's power is still the same* . . . He still will and *wants to* save sinners. Let us remember that *all things are possible with God* – so instead of looking at the dark side, let us go forward *looking unto Jesus* for victories. Instead of DECREASING our activities because times are hard, we should INCREASE our labors, our time, and our money for the salvation of souls.

Now, there is *another* class of people who live entirely in the FUTURE. These people plan to do great things in the by-and-by, but they do nothing in the *present.* Their time is taken up in planning to do something for the future. It is right to make plans in preparation for the future–but in what way can we best *prepare* for the days ahead? There is only one way–by living in and properly using the resources of the present. What we do today will be another stone in our building of the future. Those who plan only for the future and live in the future never get anything accomplished, for their future never comes. You see, *today* is *yesterday's tomorrow*–and if you do not live in the *present,* you will never catch up with your future.

Christians waste many opportunities by putting off duties until "tomorrow.'' They *intend* to do marvelous things for the Lord, but day by day they put off *doing* those "marvelous things.'' They procrastinate. *Sinners* have lost their souls and dropped into an everlasting hell because they put off salvation until "tomorrow.'' For them "tomorrow'' never came. God help each of us to do *today* what He leads us to do, to take advantage of opportunities that come to us in the *present.* "Boast not thyself of to morrow; for thou knowest not what a day may bring forth" (Prov. 27:1).

There are those in this class who do very little in the present, because they are waiting for "something to turn up in their favor." They are waiting for big opportunities to come to them. For instance, there are some people who long to go to Africa to win the heathen to Christ; yet they have never witnessed to the grocery boy, the next-door neighbor, or even to those in the slum district of their own town. They think that if they could only go to Africa, they could do great things. So there they sit, doing nothing, because the "great thing" they are looking for never happens. How foolish to waste time in this way, scorning to do the little things, waiting for something *big* to turn up. Something big *will* turn up one of these days for these people, but not what they are looking for – it will be the *judgment day*. Yes, the day will turn up, and it will turn these people up, too: "For God will bring every work into judgment, with every secret thing, whether it be good, or whether it be evil" (Ecc. 12:14).

There are others who constantly *borrow tomorrow's troubles*. Oh! How much time is spent in worrying over troubles that never come, troubles which dwell only in the imagination. I know a lady who never enjoys one thing she has because she fears she will get sick sometime in the future and will need the money for doctor bills. I do not advocate reckless spending–but why not enjoy the material blessings we have today instead of worrying over something that may never happen? Not only in the matter of money but in other things, there are people who in their imagination build a bridge somewhere in the future, the crossing of which involves pain and suffering. In their minds they are constantly crossing this bridge. Since

I was a child, I have heard this wise old saying: "Do not cross your bridges until you get to them." How easy, but how *foolish*, it is to borrow trouble; how completely it unnerves and disqualifies us for the duties and responsibilities of today. It has been said, "No man ever sank under today's burden, but it is when *tomorrow's* is added that we give way."

There is a song whose words thrill my soul each time I hear them, especially these:

> "I don't know about tomorrow;
> It may bring me poverty . . .
> But I know who holds tomorrow,
> And I know who holds my hand."

I will not worry about my tomorrows; God knows about my future, I know *Him* . . . and that is enough for me. Christ says, "Take therefore no thought for the morrow: for the morrow shall take thought for the things of itself" (Matt. 6:34). It is definitely wrong to go about weighted down with tomorrow's burdens and with things which might not come to pass, for God says, "As thy days, so shall thy strength be" (Deut. 33:25).

What are we to do then? *We are to live in the PRESENT.* We are to live a life of faith and prayer. We are to put our trust in God for every plan we form, every step we take, and every act we perform. No wonder some people are bowed down with care, for they are bearing *three kinds* of trouble—all they had in the *past*, all they have *now*, and all they may have in the *future*. In thinking of the past and the future, let us remember that we cannot really live in either; we can only live in the *present*. Let us also remember, as children of God, *we do not have to bear our burdens alone*. Jesus Christ is our Burden-Bearer. The Bible says, "Casting all your care upon Him; for He careth for you" (I Pet. 5:7).

It is right to think of the future and plan for it; it is right to think of and profit from the experiences of the past – *but we are to LIVE in the PRESENT*. Do not allow opportunities to go by today, while you wait for better ones to come tomorrow. Do not give up and sit down because of the past. By living in the present, we have to take only one step at a time, and to take that step wisely is all we have to be concerned about at this time. Those who are climbing a steep mountain concentrate on one step at a time; if they look down, they may get dizzy; if they look up toward the top, they may become discouraged. There is no Christian strong enough to bear the strain of the duties of today PLUS those of tomorrow at the same time; but when tomorrow comes, with it will come the grace and strength sufficient for that day. God gives us grace only for *today's* duties and burdens. We do not need strength for tomorrow's work today.

Many Christians worry because they do not have *dying grace*. Death to them is a great enemy, and they look toward it with fear. They are trying to cross their bridge before they get to it. They do not need dying grace right now . . . but they need grace to LIVE for the Lord and to WORK for Him. When they come to death's door, *then* God will supply the grace to die. Today, you need *living* grace; God gives abundantly of His grace for each hour and each need of every day. "And God is able to make ALL grace abound toward you; that ye, ALWAYS having ALL sufficiency in ALL things, may abound to EVERY good work" (II Cor. 9:8).

So, I remind you, God says, "*Redeem the time*." Only by living in the present can we redeem the time. The past is gone–it is fixed–and the future is God's. But the *present* is *ours*, so let us make use of it! Let us take advantage of every opportunity that comes our way, and let us *make new opportunities.* If it is getting harder to reach sinners, we must plan to *work* harder. I realize it will cost something to redeem the time it will cost thought, energy, labor, and perseverance. If we are to live in the present, taking advantage of our opportunities, we must pay the price of surrender, sacrifice, and service. As a soldier of the Lord, are you willing to go forth to battle, warring against the evil influences? Do not be a slackard. March forward ONE STEP AT A TIME, and trust the Captain of our soul to lead on to victory! Whatever the future may bring, remember that you do not have to live more than one day at a time. I beg you to let the Lord lead and give you grace for that one day.

THE WITHERED GOURD

THE WITHERED GOURD

"But God prepared a worm when the morning rose the next day, and it smote the gourd that it withered. . . And God said to Jonah, Doest thou well to be angry for the gourd? And he said, I do well to be angry, even unto death" (Jonah 4:7,9).

The Book of Jonah is a small one and the prophet of the book a disobedient, bigoted Jew; but the smallness of the book and the peculiarities of the Prophet Jonah should not cause us to lose the great lessons and divine truths infolded in the four short chapters.

Jesus Christ Himself vouched for the historical character of the man Jonah when He revealed a divine truth concerning His own death, burial, and resurrection which had been hidden for ages in the account given by Jonah. Certain of the scribes and Pharisees asked Jesus to give them a sign. He answered, "An evil and adulterous generation seeketh after a sign; and there shall no sign be given to it, but the sign of the prophet Jonas: For as Jonas was three days and three nights in the whale's belly; so shall the Son of man be three days and three nights in the heart of the earth" (Matt. 12:39,40).

If our precious Lord (who is the beginning and ending of knowledge, the first and the last letter in the alphabet—Rev. 1:8) used Jonah's experience as a sign, then *we* should not despise or ignore this prophet.

In studying Jonah we could examine many aspects of his life, but our objective in this study is to help those who have manifold burdens and are going through fiery trials of the devil. Afflictions produce a twofold effect:

they either make us more submissive to God, or they render us impatient, irritable, and rebellious. The influence of Jonah's trials upon him seems to have been of this latter character. He manifested such a murmuring and discontented spirit, one wonders why God would choose such a man to do His work.

We may marvel, but we must not question God's choice; for does not our own experience teach us that believers are often inconsistent characters? Only God could—or *would*—have such patience and longsuffering with mankind. We may well be thankful for Isaiah 55:8, which says that God's ways are not our ways, and for I Corinthians 1:27, which says, "But God hath chosen the foolish things of the world to confound the wise; and God hath chosen the weak things of the world to confound the things which are mighty."

As we note God's patience with Jonah, it should be an encouragement to us who sometimes despair with our own inabilities, inconsistencies, and failures in the Christian walk. Jonah had been sent to pronounce God's anger upon the city of Nineveh. At first he rebelled and sought passage on a ship going to Tarshish; but a storm arose, and the mariners—knowing that Jonah was the cause of God's wrath—threw him overboard. A great fish swallowed him, and three days later cast him out on dry land.

A *second* time God spoke to Jonah and told him to go to Nineveh—and this time he obeyed. He went through the city proclaiming that in forty days God would bring judgment upon Nineveh. The king and all the people *repented*, and God spared the city. This displeased Jonah. He had foretold that in forty days Nineveh would be overthrown, and he considered that the non-fulfillment of his preaching made him appear to be a false prophet. This so offended him that he wished he might die.

The natural reaction in a prophet's heart for the salvation of a city should be one of relief. His heart *should* sing for joy over the great mercy of the Lord. But Jonah was *unnatural*: he had no joy. Instead of joy, he had pity for himself and rebellion toward God. He felt that God had done him a great injustice by not destroying the city, and so deeply grieved was he over this seeming injustice that he wanted to die!

It is amazing that this merciful act of God caused Jonah to display such a spirit as to lead us to the conclusion that he would rather a great city and all its inhabitants be destroyed, than for his reputation as a prophet to be questioned. He went out on the east side of the city, built a booth, and sat down in his misery to see what would become of the city! Even then, God was merciful: He prepared a gourd and caused it to come up over Jonah, that it might be a shadow over his head *to deliver him from his grief.* The Scripture tells us that "Jonah was exceeding glad of the gourd."

But God had yet more to teach Jonah: He prepared a worm to smite the gourd that it might wither and die. He then prepared an oppressive wind to come from the east; the sun beat upon Jonah's head until he fainted; and again he wished for death.

Here we find Jonah oppressed and fainting—*but not forsaken,* for God asked him, "Doest thou well to be angry for the gourd?" Still angry and offended, Jonah replied, "I do well to be angry, even unto death!" *Did* Jonah die there on the east side of Nineveh? We are not told, for the history of Jonah stops with his last words of anger in verse 9, chapter 4. The last two verses of that chapter give God's answer to the prophet. How could Jonah answer

God in such a manner? How could he continue to be sullen and peevish toward God? I do not know the answer to that question, but I do know that Christians of his character are not uncommon even today.

As we study about this prophet who wanted to die because God spared a city and smote a gourd vine, let us notice that:

1. **Jonah's grief was unreasonable.** His prayer for death was born from anger, not from reason, and he behaved no better than a spoiled child who throws down his toys and refuses to play if he cannot have his own way. No sooner were Jonah's wishes crossed than he broke forth in sullen complaint. He wished to die merely because God had spared Nineveh and he feared that as a result his own reputation would suffer. The amazing part of the entire episode is that he took this unreasonable attitude. Instead of anger and depression it would have been more in line with human nature for him to have been tempted in the *opposite* direction—toward an attitude of *pride*. He could have become proud of himself and of what HE had accomplished *through HIS wonderful preaching*!

If Jonah had stood on a hillside, looked out over the city and said, "Look what *I* have done! I saved a whole city from destruction," we could understand his attitude, even though we might not approve of it; nor could we blame him had he felt that the people of Nineveh should bless him forever for his part in their salvation. But instead of this *natural* line of reasoning, he took the unnatural. Because of his concern for his reputation (which he considered ruined) he could not see the good which had been accomplished.

Jonah's attitude is not unfamiliar, even in our lives. How often, when a poor old sinner is saved, is the remark made, "He will not stay sober for six weeks!" And when the six weeks have passed and the saved one is still living for God, the person who made the statement and those who agreed to it seem disappointed and vexed because their prediction did not come true! Jonah wished to die, to enter the realms of eternity and stand before his God, merely because of the trivial incident of a withered gourd which he did not plant and for which he did not labor.

This withered gourd has often puzzled me. I realize that teachers of the Word give the book of Jonah a prophetic meaning; but I believe that all Scripture has a primary and a secondary interpretation, and therefore I do not see why we are not to receive a practical as well as a *prophetic* lesson from Jonah's experience.

In verse 5 of chapter 4 we learn that Jonah built a booth and sat in the *shadow* of it. Why then did God prepare a *gourd* to be a shadow over his head? You will notice that the gourd was "*to deliver him from his grief,*" and we know that it accomplished its purpose temporarily, for Jonah was "*exceeding glad*" for it. We could say that the lesson was to show that Jonah tried to find relief outside of God and without God's help when he built the booth – and this we could back up with Scripture showing that we should always rest in the shadow of the Almighty (Psalm 91:1; Lam. 4:20).

However, if that is the meaning of the prepared gourd, we then run into difficulty; for the very next day God prepared a worm to cut the gourd down! This does not sound like our loving heavenly Father–to *give*, then immediately *take away*–if He were teaching Jonah to look to *Him* for comfort and relief instead of trusting in the labor of his own hands. James 1:17 says, "Every good gift and every perfect gift is from above, and cometh down from the

Father of lights, with whom is *no variableness, neither shadow of turning.*" Romans 11:29 tells us that "the gifts and calling of God are without repentance." So surely we must look for another meaning of the gourd vine, which God gave and immediately took away.

I think the answer is in God's words to Jonah in the last two verses of the book:

"Then said the Lord, Thou hast had pity on the gourd. for the which thou hast not laboured, neither madest it grow; which came up in a night, and perished in a night: and should not I spare Nineveh, that great city, wherein are more than sixscore thousand persons that cannot discern between their right hand and their left hand; and also much cattle?"

God was trying to show His prophet that while he had had pity on a gourd–an earthly possession that would soon vanish away–he had had no pity for the people of Nineveh whose souls would never die. Jonah's continued anger and failure to repent in the face of God's illustrated sermon is almost unbelievable. But why do we condemn Jonah when we constantly find *ourselves* putting great emphasis on shadows rather than emphasizing the lasting *substance*?

How often do we fret over the material things of life and forget the important salvation of souls? Material things vanish away as did the gourd, but that which is done for Christ will last forever. Day by day we meet people whose souls will be living somewhere a million years from now, and our words, our lives, or our actions may determine where those souls will spend eternity. Yet in the face of this tremendous truth and responsibility we spend more time planning, worrying, and praying for material things than for the eternal souls of our neighbors.

Is it possible that we do not believe God when He

says, "Seek ye first the kingdom of God, and His righteousness; and all these things shall be added unto you" (Matt. 6:33)? Or do we simply *forget* this promise because of the weakness of the flesh as we become enmeshed with daily tasks? In Philippians 4:6 the Word tells us, "Be careful for nothing; but in every thing by prayer and supplication with thanksgiving let your requests be made known unto God." Do not worry or fret over the needs of the flesh. Work and plan—yes; but trust God through it all. He has promised to supply all of our needs. Be diligent in work, and trust Him for increase. Christians should not worry, fret, and plan to the exclusion of the spiritual needs for themselves and for others.

How senseless and unreasonable was Jonah's grief! First he grieved over the salvation of a city full of people, and then he grieved over a withered gourd. Little did he value the precious life God had given him. Just suppose God had taken him at his word when he asked to die. How would he have felt when he stood before God? Would he not have been ashamed of such a prayer, and of his complaining and bitterness over so small a trial in the work God gave him to do?

In our *own* lives, too, it would pay us to stop and think before we allow ourselves to be given to complaints. Often, after we have been disturbed and upset, after we have cried and complained, we have had to admit that we demonstrated more anger, grief, or discouragement than the occasion called for. When we look back over a trial in which we have completely given way, we can see the unreasonableness of our actions. God talked with Jonah and tried to make him see the irrationality of his grief; but the prophet still insisted that he "did well" to be angry, and that he was right in wishing to die. In the time of *our* trials and heartaches God also talks to *us*. He speaks to us through His Word, saying, "My grace is sufficient for thee" (II Cor. 12:9). He gives us comfort and assurance by saying, "Beloved, think it not strange concerning the fiery trial which is to try you, as though some strange thing happened unto you: BUT REJOICE, inasmuch as ye are partakers of Christ's sufferings; that, when His glory shall be revealed, ye may be glad also with exceeding joy" (I Pet. 4:12,13). Psalm 30:5 tells us that "weeping may endure for a night, but joy cometh in the morning."

Every burden God places upon us—or allows to *be* placed upon us—is for our good. He knows exactly what it will take to bring us into complete sympathy with Himself. When He allows burdens and afflictions to come upon us it is our duty to bear them with perfect resignation to His will. He not only *knows* what is best – He *DOES* what is best. Let us also bear in mind that there is never a burden placed upon us without God, at the same time, giving us grace and strength to bear it. With every *burden* come love, encouragement, and strength from the Father's hand. Just when we think the trials are too many and too heavy, God places His everlasting arms underneath us and bears us up! "Many are the afflictions of the righteous: *but the Lord delivereth him out of them all*" (Psa. 34:19).

But regardless of His strong assurance that He will bear us up in time of trial and tribulation, we often chafe under our burdens and make matters worse by saying that we have a *right* to be discouraged! Many Christians become so bitter in time of trial that they make the age-old complaint, "God puts more on me than I can bear." Such accusation against God is selfish and unjust; for even while the discouraged one is floundering in his bitterness and self-pity, God is trying to reason with him even as He did with Jonah: "*There hath no temptation taken you but such as is common to man: but God is faithful, who will not suffer you to be tempted above that ye are able; but will with the temptation also make a way to escape, THAT YE MAY BE ABLE TO BEAR IT*" (I Cor. 10:13).

When we are *oppressed* or *depressed*, we should be careful what we say. When we feel as Jonah did we are unable to see things in proper perspective, and at such times we may make statements of which we afterward must repent. Especially should we be careful of expressing a desire to die. This is a very *cowardly* thing to do. Many times I have heard people, troubled and burdened, say, "O that I could die!" Such a statement is most often born of self-pity. These people feel sorry for themselves and they want others to think that they are in the extremity of burdens and trials. Because they are cowards, they do not want to gracefully bear the inconveniences that come their way. They think only of getting out from under them; and as soon as the depression is past and everything looks bright again, they forget their desire to die. I wonder if they even remember to *thank* God for not taking them at their word when they made such a foolish wish for death?

Some people are so morbid they cannot think or talk of anything except the relief it will bring for them to be put in the grave! They claim that life is cruel and that for them it holds no joys. Therefore they speak of the grave as "a sweet resting place." Do these people actually think that such words make others believe that they are extraordinary saints who live very close to God? If they do think this, they are sadly mistaken. Christians should not be *afraid* to die – but neither should they be afraid to *live*!

The Apostle Paul was persecuted from the time he was saved until he died. Not only was he persecuted by his fellowman, but he was also bearing *a thorn in the flesh* which God did not see fit to remove. Yet so great was his courage that from a prison cell he wrote to the Philippians, "I am in a strait betwixt two, having a desire to depart, and to be with Christ; which is far better: *Nevertheless to abide in the flesh is more needful for you*" (Phil. 1:23,24). We who are saved have work to do. God is not calling on us to die for Him, but to *live* for Him. Paul's desire to "depart and be with Christ" was not the product of a bitter, discouraged heart. He could make that statement because he was near the end of his life and he could honestly testify, "I have fought a good fight, I have finished my course, I have kept the faith" (II Tim. 4:7). Paul was not, like Jonah (and like many Christians today), guilty of wishing to die because he was irritated or discouraged over some trial that had come his way.

It matters not how pious may be your talk about the grave, it cannot be gilded over with morbid wishes for it. Death is an enemy, and it is only in looking *beyond* death and the grave that the Christian finds hope–a hope that is anchored in the blessed promise of abiding forever in the presence of our Lord. The morbid Christians who talk so sentimentally about the grave as "a quiet resting place" are not looking beyond it to an eternity with Jesus! If they had their eyes on HIM they would be busy about the Father's business. By God's grace they would be able to bear up under trial, trusting all things to their Saviour. If you will observe these modern Jonahs you will find that they never wish to die when all things are going well. It is only when things are not going their way that they become discontented and say they want to die. If they expressed a desire to go on home to be with the Lord when everything was well with them, we might be led to believe that they truly *are* anxious to go to be with Him. But since in the majority of cases this desire to die is present only in times of trial, I conclude that they are weary of their *pains*, not of their *sins*; and that they long to die because they are sick of life, *not because they expect happiness in God.*

Heaven should not be entered in such a frame of mind as this. Those who most passionately wish for the grave are sometimes most unfit for it. They may paint beautiful pictures of being released from their cares – but a far more beautiful picture is that of one who is *casting all his care upon the Lord* and keeping busy winning souls for his Saviour. Christians should remember the admonition given in Hebrews 12:3: "For *consider Him* that endured such contradiction of sinners against Himself, lest ye be wearied and faint in your minds."

2. **Jonah's grief showed a rebellious spirit.** He was not willing to have God's will in his life. He resisted, even when God saved a great city and all its inhabitants. When *we* murmur against our lot in life, it shows the same rebellious spirit in us, as though our plans were better than *God's* plans. We condemn Jonah for wanting "hell fire and brimstone" to fall upon Nineveh, we can see that he was in the wrong in being angry with God for sparing the city; yet sometimes we are blind to our own rebellious spirit. We must admit that we are not always submissive to God's way, and we murmur against Him who holds our very breath of life in His hands!

Some people try to justify their rebellious spirit and excuse their complaining by accusing God of dealing unfairly with them. One person will say, "I could bear my ill health if it were not that this sickness prevents my serving God." He complains that he is not able to visit the poor, wait on the sick, and render various other services in the church. Thus he uses his supposed zeal for the Lord's work as an excuse for rebelling against the path God has laid out for him. He does not stop to realize that if God had wanted him to do these services, He would have made it *possible* for him to do them. What God demands, God also provides; and when He calls upon one of His servants to accomplish a work for Him, He orders the necessary equipment to fulfill that work—whether that equipment be faith, grace, courage, wisdom, health, or money. All heaven and its hosts are at the disposal of that saint whom God designates to serve in any given task. Is He not then able to supply OUR every need? Is He not capable of setting the course which is best for us?

The flesh is weak and cannot be trusted. If good health were given to the sick person who complains because he cannot work in the church, could he be sure that he would expend his energies in that channel? He might instead use his strength and health in worldly pursuits. Of one thing we can be sure: We can trust God fully and know that what He does in our life is for our good and His eternal glory.

How prone Christians are to make their zeal for serving God an excuse for becoming rebellious against His appointment of a place for them to serve. There are those who grieve and grumble because they do not have the talent to sing or play an instrument—and they envy those who *can* do these things. Still others rebel when they are placed in certain positions in God's house, because they want to do another (and what *they* consider a *greater*) work.

But such a believer should study the admonition given

to the Corinthian Christians by the Apostle Paul. The Church is a body made up of many members, and all members are necessary. There are no "little" members, no "little" ministries. All service is *great* if it is God-appointed and if it is rendered to the *glory* of God. Even a cup of cold water given in the name of Jesus is not overlooked in the heavenly record.

In I Corinthians 12:12–31 Paul points out the parallel between the human body and the Church of the living God. Each member of the body is important and necessary. The body is ONE, but has many members; and so is the *Church* one body with many members. Paul declares that *God* has set the members–*every one of them*–in the body "AS IT HATH PLEASED HIM" (v. 18). In verses 22–24 he points out that "those members of the body, which seem to be more feeble, are *necessary*: and those members of the body, *which WE think to be less honourable*, upon these we bestow more abundant honour. . . GOD HATH TEMPERED THE BODY TOGETHER, having given more abundant honour to that part which lacked." In verses 26 and 27 he points out that when *one* member suffers, *all the members suffer with it*; and when *one* member is honored, *all the members REJOICE with it*! "Now ye are the body of Christ, and members in particular."

Therefore–whether chairman of the board, janitor, organist, Sunday school superintendent, or secretary of the smallest class–*we are workers together WITH Christ, FOR Christ, and to the HONOR OF HIS NAME.* There are no little jobs when we work for Jesus. Regardless of how insignificant our assigned task may seem to US, if it brings glory to His name we should count it a God-given privilege to serve Him. We should do with diligence and a true heart whatever task is ours. We serve GOD, not man; and

GOD, not man, will reward us. If we are faithful in our service we will receive a FULL reward (II John 8).

Our duty is to submit to God's appointments and not try to dictate to Him. In whatever place He chooses for us, we should be able to say with Paul, "*. . . I have learned, in whatsoever state I am, therewith to be content*" (Phil. 4:11). In I Timothy 6:6 we are told that "godliness with contentment is great gain."

Let us assure our hearts over and over again that God knows best. When we are tempted to complain because of trials, let us look into the future and consider that we will be living *somewhere forever*! Our life on earth is *so short* when compared with the eternities ahead. This life is but a "preparation time" for where we will spend those millions of years. If trials and disappointments are part of our preparation, then let us not complain; rather, let us trust completely in God. He can see into the eternities ahead, and He knows us better than we know ourselves. Paul tells us, "For our light affliction, which is but for a moment, worketh for us a far more exceeding and eternal weight of glory; while we look not at the things which are seen, but at the things which are not seen: for the things which are seen are temporal; but the things which are not seen are eternal" (II Cor. 4:17,18).

It has been so aptly said that when a Christian has "*dis*appointment," he should change the first letter to "h" and thus it would be "*His appointment*." Let us rest securely in His love and do the best we can with whatever means we have at our disposal, however limited. Remember, the little lad in John 6 had only five loaves and two fishes—but his meager store, surrendered to Jesus, fed more than five thousand hungry people, with plenty to spare! God can take so little, and—when yielded to Him—

multiply it into abundance beyond what we are able to think or plan.

Mary had only a bottle of perfume to give to Jesus; but she took it and anointed His feet, and His commendation of her was, "*She hath done what she could*!" Can we say the same for ourselves? When the believer *does what he CAN* in the service of the Lord—service that brings glory to Jesus rather than praise to man—that believer will receive a full reward. It is not the *size* of the ministry or service, but the *faithfulness* with which it is rendered. "Every man's work shall be made manifest . . . because it shall be revealed by fire; and the fire shall try every man's work of what SORT it is" (I Cor. 3:12–15).

3. Jonah was selfish. When Jonah preached "coming destruction" to the people of Nineveh, everyone—from king to lowest peasant—put on sackcloth and ashes, a token of humility and repentance. This unusual scene of an entire city in repentance was such that surely the angels rejoiced as they looked down upon it. But Jonah was so deeply absorbed in his petty trials—the withering of a gourd vine and the danger of losing his reputation as a prophet—that he saw nothing over which to rejoice! The saving of thousands of souls gave him no pleasure, and by his own actions he proved that he would have had the entire city perish rather than have his prophecy proved untrue.

Do we have selfish "Jonahs" today? Most definitely we do. We find selfish men even in pulpits today who *for personal gain* are selling out all that they once held dear—denying the Word of God and leading men, women, and children astray. In order to rank high in their denomination they are willing for their congregation to go to hell. *How else* are we to interpret their actions? At one time some of these men preached the Gospel and were interested in souls. Now they have climbed the ladder of success and their people grope in darkness—*church members, but LOST*!

And what are many of *God's children* doing? Some are, figuratively speaking, mourning over a withered gourd. Some are angry, nursing a grudge because someone whispered adverse things about them, criticized their motives, or questioned their Christian life. Still others have been hindered from having their own way, or perhaps could not get others to cooperate with them, and therefore they sit on the sidelines saying with Jonah, "I do well to be angry." They are pouting over *small* matters while great opportunities pass them by! An *outward* look will reveal unto us the thousands of lost souls rushing pell-mell into an eternity without God, and an *inward* look will reveal our terrible selfishness in sitting around feeling sorry for ourselves and doing nothing about winning the lost.

The next time you are grieved or despondent, ask yourself *WHY* you are so moved. Is it for your soul's welfare? Is it for the glory of God? Is it for salvation of the lost? *These* are worthy of your concern; but in times of trial *do not waste your grief over a withered gourd*! These are times when born again children of God need to *stand* together and *fight* together against the common foe. This is not the time for each of us to go off and sit down under our separate gourd vines to pout over hurt feelings, imagined wrongs, and selfish motives. Such an attitude is, like that of Jonah, only sympathy for self.

4. Jonah's attitude was one of unbelief. God had brought His prophet up from the depths of the sea, He had delivered him out of the belly of the whale. Could that same God not be trusted to take care of Jonah's reputation and provide for his comfort? If the king of Nineveh and his people had so much confidence in Jonah as a prophet as to heed his words of warning and repent, would they be likely to despise him as a *false* prophet after God spared them through his preaching? Would they not gladly have received him into their homes and provided every need for his comfort?

The whole city, humbled before God, presented a wonderful opportunity for Jonah to instruct the people and perfect the work of reformation! But instead of using the open door of the Ninevites, Jonah passed through the city in unbelief.

Such frail and imperfect creatures were even the prophets of God (if there can be any comfort in such a thought); and just so distrustful and rebellious are we! In times of trial we forget the many times God has intervened in our behalf, the times He has upheld us with His right hand. We forget to sing:

"Through many dangers, toils, and snares,
I have already come;
'Tis grace hath brought me safe thus far,
And grace will lead me home!"

Indeed, we must admit that we are ofttimes distrustful, anxious, and rebellious in times of trials and afflictions. Oh, for a firmer faith, that we may be able to say with Job, "*Though He slay me, yet will I trust in Him*!"

We have seen that impatient grief is rebellious, unreasonable, selfish, and unbelieving–yet which of us can say that we have not acted as Jonah did? We may have such perfect command of ourselves as to keep our rebellion from being made manifest to others, but we cannot deny that we *have had* these impatient, selfish feelings. The Bible tells us that it is the little foxes that spoil the vines, and yielding to impatience over worthless "gourds" robs many Christians of their joy and of their worth to

God in service. If we would only look to Him and trust Him in the little things that annoy us, we would be stronger and more capable of standing *greater* trials without fainting or complaining.

We shall find, too, that the less we *speak* of our crosses and the less we meditate upon them, the more they will diminish in size and the easier they can be borne or overcome. Jonah went out and *sat down* – and while the heat and the wind were beating upon him outwardly, he was feeding the fire of discontent within himself; and his impatience at last broke forth in his saying that he wanted to die. Had he been busy praising God and giving out the Word, he would not have come to such a state of anger and depression.

May God help you to trust Him completely, and to "think it not strange concerning the fiery trial which is to try you, as though some strange thing happened unto you" (I Pet. 4:12).

GROWTH IN FAITH

GROWTH IN FAITH

In John 4:46–54 we have the account of the healing of the nobleman's son. In this portion of Scripture we have a good example of weak faith which becomes strong. Many people complain of having weak faith, but do not know what to do about it. I trust that from this study of the nobleman we can see just where his faith was weak, and how weak faith may become strong.

First, what are THE SIGNS OF WEAK FAITH?

1. Demanding Visible Proof.

When the nobleman "heard that Jesus was come out of Judaea into Galilee, he went unto Him, and besought Him that He would come down, and heal his son; for he was at the point of death. Then said Jesus unto him, *Except ye see signs and wonders, ye will not believe.*" It is human nature to desire to see something. There is an old saying, "Seeing is believing"; yet it has been proven many times that we can be deceived by sight. Witnesses have sworn that they saw a certain person at the scene of a crime, and later it was proven to be a case of mistaken identity. A man in Greenville declared he saw a deacon going into a place of worldly amusement, though the deacon was in reality going into the doctor's office *next door.* The man's sight had deceived him. *Faith based upon sight is very weak faith.* "The devils believe and tremble." They see evidences of God's power which they cannot deny, and they tremble before it . . . but the devils are certainly not saved. The world says, "Seeing is believing"—but *faith* says, "*Believing is seeing.*" It is really *unbelief* which demands visible proof. *Thomas* said, "I will not believe until I *see*." Jesus rebuked him and said, "Blessed are they that have not seen, and yet believe."

The rich man in hell said, "Send someone to tell my five brethren not to come to this place of torment . . . if one rise from the dead, they will believe." "NO," said Abraham, "If they hear not Moses and the prophets, neither will they be persuaded though one rose from the dead."

There are a lot of people today who demand visible proof – miracles, something to see – "And then," they say, "I will believe." No, according to God's Word, they would not believe then. If they will not believe the Bible and recognize the miracles of God's grace all around them, actually *seeing* something would not help. The more they rely on sight, the weaker is their faith and the more they demand to see.

God wants us to believe Him as He speaks through the Word. Yet people say, "God, you said it . . . but I cannot accept your *Word* – so prove to me by some visible sign . . . something that I can see . . . that you have kept your Word."

It is lack of faith that Paul speaks of in I Corinthians 14:22. He says, "Wherefore tongues are for a sign, not to them that believe, but to them that believe not." He is talking to born again believers *only* here, and he divides them into two groups – "those saints who believe" and "those saints who *believe not*." Dr. DeHaan, in his exposition on the book of Corinthians, has such a wonderful explanation that I want to give it to you. I quote: "Two different words are used in the Greek. The word used in the first phrase, 'tongues are for a sign, not to them that believe . . .' is the word *pisteuo*, which denotes full confidence and trust. In the second instance, in the phrase, 'but to them that believe not . . .' the word is *apistos*, and means 'one who does not fully trust.' It may be translated 'doubter,' so that the passage would naturally read, 'Wherefore tongues are for a sign, not to them (who fully trust the Lord), but to them (who still doubt).'"

Those people who had weak faith wanted a sign – but signs are unnecessary for those who fully believe God and take Him at His Word.

2. Another sign of weak faith and of a weak Christian is that: **He Must Be Driven to God by a Desperate Need.**

The nobleman's son was at the point of death. No doubt the father had called in every doctor that he knew, and all of them had given up the case as hopeless. In this time of great distress, when all else had failed, *he thought of Jesus*! It is like the numbers of others who have "reached the end of the rope" and called out, "Lord, have mercy on me," because all else has failed. Such faith is better than *no* faith – but not as good as the faith that draws us to God by love and gratitude. It is better to be *driven* than not to come at all . . . but why wait until tragedy strikes, to turn to God? It is so much better to be in close contact with God, trusting Him, resting on Him, living for Him at all times – and then when the "valley experiences" come, they are not borne alone.

No doubt the nobleman had heard Jesus many times, but did not go to Him or invite Him to his house. Surely he *must* have previously heard Jesus, to have enough faith to call Him to his dying son. It was *weak* faith, exercised only because of a great need – but at least it was *some* faith. *Zacchaeus* invited the Lord to dine with him when there was no sorrow to be relieved. Such faith seems to me to be *greater* faith than that which drives us by sheer force to seek Jesus.

3. A third sign of weak faith is that: **While It Prays, It Dictates to God.**

In verse 49 the nobleman said, "Sir, COME DOWN ere my child die." Notice that he did not make his request known to Jesus – and then leave the rest to the One who doeth all things well. He said, "COME DOWN and heal my son." He dictated to Jesus just what he wanted Him to do. We know that all Jesus had to do was to speak a word, and the son would be healed; He did not have to go down to the house to accomplish the needs of this nobleman. Then, too, if Jesus *had* answered this father's prayer exactly as he dictated, the child could have died while He *went down.* The nobleman lived in *Capernaum,* and Jesus was in *Cana of Galilee.* The child was at the point of death when the father left, and could easily have died while the father made the journey to Cana and back again with Jesus.

Perfect faith does not dictate to God, but has trust in the perfect wisdom of God. How often we find ourselves asking God for things–and dictating to Him the way it is to be done! It will be a wonderful day in our Christian life when we, with simple faith, trust God to answer our petitions when and how He pleases. In infinite love and mercy, and by His perfect wisdom, He will work all things out for our good and for His glory. But I am afraid that much of our praying consists of dictating to God *where* and *when* and *how* to answer our prayers. Then, if the answer does not come according to our specifications, we lose hope, doubting that God even heard our petition.

4. The fourth sign of weak faith is: **Impatience.**

"Sir, come down ere my child die." There is evidence here of a short temper. The nobleman thinks this is no time to argue or to explain. What he wants is haste. There

seems also to be a bit of arrogance here on the part of the nobleman. He has not forgotten that he is among the nobility, and he is giving orders accordingly. Perhaps he feels as did the chief priests and Pharisees when they said, "Have any of the rulers of the Pharisees believed on Him?" They implied that only the *rabble* had followed Jesus–not the learned men or those in higher society. At any rate, the father wanted haste . . . he was impatient.

There are times when *we* are impatient for *our* prayers to be answered–and should God heed our impatient begging, it would not be for our good. A girl was begging God to give her a job. She set a deadline and earnestly begged God to answer her prayer. That special day, she went for an interview, begging God all the time in her heart, "Give me this job." But . . . she was refused, and returned home quite dejected. From necessity, she started out again the next morning, trying to find work. That day a much better position was opened to her, and then she realized that had God listened to her dictating the day before, she would have had "second best."

Another girl told me that when she was first courting, she thought she was desperately in love with a boy, and prayed earnestly for God to give him to her for a husband. However, in infinite mercy and love, God did not answer her prayer. Later He gave to her a much better husband – and she says she thanks Him every day for taking care of her when she did not have the wisdom to care for herself. She was blinded by her affection for a boy whom she now does not even respect.

Oh, when will we realize that God knows more than we do and that He wants the best for His children! It is comforting, however, to know that Jesus honors even such faith as this. Though impatient, dictatorial, driven by need, and seeking visible proof, He answered the prayer of this father. He pities our weakness. How we should love and worship such a Saviour!

A preacher tells of an experience he had. Sitting in a church one morning, he heard a hoarse, discordant voice behind him, and regretted the fact that he was so near such a disagreeable singer. The song leader announced a hymn, "Just As I Am, Without One Plea"–and the discordant voice, without any melody or tune, followed the words through. While the interlude was being played, the preacher felt a hand touch his arm, and the rough voice said, "Please, sir . . . what is the next verse? Tell me the first line, and I think I can remember the rest." "Just as I am, poor, wretched, blind . . ." said the preacher – and as he looked into the stranger's face, he saw that he was blind! When he heard that grating voice trying to sing the next lines –

> "Sight, riches, healing of the mind;
> Yea, all I need in Thee to find,
> O, Lamb of God! I come; I come." –

the preacher said he felt that he would like to lend the man what voice *he* had and help him to sing, if he could have. And so God feels toward *us* when we try to serve or believe. He would help us in our failures–and, unlike this preacher, *He is able to do so.* He can give us just what we need. Jesus Christ honored the weak faith of the nobleman in order that his weak faith might become strong.

This leads us, second, to THE SIGNS OF A STRONG FAITH.

1. The first sign is: **Faith in the Word of God.**

Verse 50 tells us that "the man believed the word that Jesus had spoken unto him." He no longer desired a sign; he could now rely upon the simple Word of God. Coming into personal contact with Jesus and hearing His Word, caused the nobleman to have stronger faith. "Faith cometh by hearing, and hearing by the Word of God." So, there is something in this Word – a *living* something which goes with it and helps us to believe. The Bible is different from any other book on the face of the earth. It is vital, it is living – and this fact is impressed upon those who read it.

I reverence the Bible as a Book, but I do not hold superstitious feelings toward it as some people do. I do not regard its binding, paper, and ink as especially sacred; *the TRUTH in it* is the sacred thing. Many people worship the Book itself, and feel terribly guilty if they should accidentally drop it . . . yet they drop most of the promises and truths of the Bible out of their lives through unbelief and never give it a thought. They are like the man who was given a prescription by the doctor, and was told to take a little of it every three hours. The next day the man was worse, and the doctor asked him if he had taken the prescription as directed. He replied, "Yes, sir"–and showed him a glass where he had put *the prescription itself* in a glass of water, and had taken a little of the water every three hours! Instead of doing what the prescription said, he took the prescription itself. In that sense, "the letter killeth." Reverence for the paper, ink, and binding of the Bible is not enough . . . it is the *truth* of the Bible that is hallowed ground. A wise reverence for the Book itself is certainly not out of place, but the point that I am trying to impress upon you is this: What the Book *means* is more than the Book itself.

Jesus said to this father, "Go thy way; thy son liveth." And he *believed what the Lord said* . . . no proof, no signs, and no written contracts. In this day of chaos, this day of rockets and modernized living, there is *one sure thing* to which we can anchor, and that is *the Word of God.* It is sure, unchangeable, and forever settled in heaven.

When I say, "The Word," I am not talking about any of the new modernized translations, either. The modernists can talk until they are blue in the face–but they will never convince me that the modern translations are just as good and probably as accurate as the King James Version. No matter what arguments they may use regarding the fallacy of the King James Version of the Bible, I still will not be disturbed or moved. They can tell me over and over again that the King James Version was translated by men such as we are, and who were not as learned as modern translators – but none of this will cause me to change my mind. If modern translations were backed by the Spirit of God, they would not need revising so often. Psalm 119:89 says: "For ever, O Lord, thy Word is *settled in heaven.*" All hell shall not prevail against God and His Word. His Word is a sure foundation, a sure anchor . . . and we can depend upon it!

Never until we get to heaven will we understand the great importance of the Word of God. Every phase of our Christian living points to the Word. All we know about God, Jesus, and the Holy Spirit is found in the pages of the Holy Bible. All we know about heaven, hell, and the hereafter, we find in the Bible. It is through the Bible that we learn we are sinners, bound for a sinner's hell . . . also that there is a Saviour to save us, and how we may be saved. After we are saved through the Word, it is through the Word that we have victorious Christian living. "And this is the victory that overcometh the world, even our faith" (I John 5:4).

2. Another sign of strong faith is: **Restfulness.**

This father came from home in great haste, and he was impatient at the delay of Jesus; but after Jesus had said, "Thy son liveth" . . . after he *believed* what Jesus said . . . we find him in no hurry. The encyclopedia says that it was only fifteen miles from Capernaum to Cana. Jesus healed the boy at the seventh hour(verse 52)—which, according to Jewish time, was one o'clock in the afternoon. Had he rushed home, he could have been there before dark – but we find that he did not return until the next day. Certainly he was *resting upon the promise of Jesus* that his boy was healed. He was so confident that all was well at home, that he felt no need to rush home to verify the fact that the boy was really well. I do not know what he did during the interim, but my guess is that he stayed around to hear more teaching from the lips of Jesus.

In Isaiah 26:3 we are told: "Thou wilt keep him in perfect peace, whose mind is stayed on thee: because he trusteth in thee." There has never been such an age of hurry as there is today; but we, too, can rest in the promises of God. "He that believeth shall not make haste" (Isaiah 28:16).

3. A third sign of strong faith is: **It's Readiness to Receive God's Answers as from GOD, and Not Give Credit to Anyone Else.**

When the servants met the nobleman and told him that his son lived, it was the very echo of what Jesus had said to him in Cana the day before. The father was ready to receive it as *a miracle from the hand of God*, because he was very careful to compare the time of the healing to the very time when Jesus had said the words, "Thy son liveth." Sometimes when we have a prayer answered, unbelief whispers in our ear, "This might have happened anyway." Or, "This is a remarkable coincidence, and would have happened even if you had not prayed for it." But strong faith stands ready to give God the praise and to confirm to others by testimony that it was a direct answer to prayer.

4. The last sign of strong faith that I will mention is: **Willingness to Receive Spiritual Blessings.**

We are told that the nobleman "himself believed, and all his house." He went to Jesus seeking temporal blessings, the healing of a body – but he received *much more.* He received the healing of his soul. Such is God's way of dealing. He knows how to give *above* all we ask or think.

I now appeal to every one of you who have been blessed of God in body, in family, in any respect. Will you not in gratitude give your hearts to Christ if you are not saved? And if you *are* saved, will you not fully give Him your life, your all?

The faith that seeks the spiritual is greater faith than that which seeks only the temporal. Where do you stand? God help you to check up . . . and spiritually to *grow up*!

TEACH US TO PRAY

TEACH US TO PRAY

"And it came to pass, that, as He was praying in a certain place, when He ceased, one of His disciples said unto Him, Lord, teach us to pray . . ." (Luke 11:1).

It is a universal fact that Christians realize the worth of prayer. Even the youngest Sunday school student can quote, "Prayer changes things"—and not only can he *quote* it—he *believes* it!

From my earliest remembrance of Sunday school and church I recall the admonition, "Read your Bible and *pray*." Even sinners expect Christians to pray – but *do we* pray? Do we really know how to pray? In my early Christian life I had no doubt that I knew how to pray – but as I have grown older I have asked myself often, "Do I *really* pray?"

My soul cries out as did the apostles', "Lord, *teach me* to pray!" In the following Scriptures we learn that we are not only supposed to pray, but we are *commanded* to do so:

Ephesians 6:18: "Praying always with all prayer and supplication in the Spirit, and watching thereunto with all perseverance and supplication for all saints."

Luke 18:1: "And He spake a parable unto them to this end, that men ought always to pray, and not to faint."

I Thessalonians 5:17: "Pray without ceasing."

James 5:16: "Confess your faults one to another, and *pray one for another,* that ye may be healed. The effectual fervent prayer of a righteous man availeth much."

I doubt that any Christian needs to be convinced that he should pray, and most Christians realize the far-reaching results of fervent prayer. Great men have written whole books on the subject—especially on the *power* of prayer. Bible classes spend weeks in the study of prayer, and I believe this is one phase of the Christian life which, to some degree, is advocated by all churches.

But with all of the available help, admonition, and teaching, some of the most conscientious Christians find themselves defeated in their prayer life and often cry out with the disciples, "Lord, *teach us to pray!*"

Upon examining this portion of Scripture in Luke, I am so glad to find that the Lord did not rebuke His disciples for their request. Surely then, the request was in order, because our Lord gave them a model prayer—an example which they could follow.

Certainly this was not a prayer that they were to quote every time they prayed, for in Matthew 6:7 He clearly instructed them, "Use not vain repetitions, as the heathen do." He was teaching them the *form* of prayer.

I realize that the model prayer given by Jesus to His disciples is a model prayer *for the Kingdom*, but most Scriptures have a primary application and a secondary application. I think if you will carefully study this model prayer you will find, in its secondary application, that it includes a great deal. It does not stretch the meaning to say that it touches on about every phase of prayer for us today:

"*Our Father which art in heaven, Hallowed be thy name*" includes the honor and worship due the heavenly Father.

"*Thy kingdom come. Thy will be done in earth, as it is in heaven*" includes belief in the supreme reign of Christ over all creation, and teaches us to pray as did John in The Revelation, "Even so, come, Lord Jesus";

for the sooner He comes in the Rapture, the nearer we are to the eternal kingdom.

"*Give us this day our daily bread*" takes care of our temporal needs.

"*And forgive us our debts, as we forgive our debtors*" sets forth our need to pray for forgiveness and that we should include others in our prayer.

"*And lead us not into temptation, but deliver us from evil*" includes our spiritual needs.

When we stop to consider that prayer is talking to God on the basis of our relationship to Jesus Christ it seems rather odd that we *need* to be taught. Prayer should come to us as naturally as the process of breathing. We who are saved are as close to God as we are to our own heart—"*Christ in you*, the hope of glory." Proverbs 18:24 tells us that He "sticketh closer than a brother," and in Psalm 46:1 we read that He is "a very present help in trouble."

Then why the *defeat* in our prayer life? And why do we need to be *taught to pray*? Of course, the greatest hindrance is our adversary, the devil. He does all that he can do to hinder us from praying and to distract our minds and hearts from God. Sometimes our physical condition hinders us; a run-down, nervous, sick body is not conducive to a prayer life. Whether it should be so or not, it is true that our spiritual feelings depend to a great degree upon our *physical* feelings.

Our own flesh (our human nature) rebels against praying. Prayer requires effort and will power and, above all, a heart that feels the *need* of prayer. "Where there is no vision, the people perish" (Prov. 29:18).

The flesh being weak and the devil doing his best to hinder our prayer life, it becomes easy to "say" a stereotyped prayer to ease the conscience. And who is the loser? YOU are, if you are guilty. Real praying does require effort—but it pays off, for it produces joy, peace, the blessedness of a closeness to God, and victory over the world!

No true believer is satisfied with a prayerless life—and even if he *could be* satisfied, *God* would not be pleased with a Christian who deliberately disobeys His command to pray. The Lord would first convict and trouble His child who failed to pray, and would finally have to chastise the son who continued to ignore His warning.

I believe that all Christians who are defeated in their prayer life desire to be taught how to pray—and I am not speaking of being taught how to stand up in public and make a "pretty prayer" in great words or "flowery" phrases. I am speaking of what the disciples asked of Jesus. Had they asked in the wrong spirit, or had their request been conceived from selfish motives, the Lord would have rebuked them as He did the Pharisees for their public prayers (Matt. 6:5).

There are many Scriptures on prayer, and many avenues through which we could examine prayer; but without becoming technical and involved in a deep theological study, let us see why we, like the disciples, need to be taught how to pray.

I.

We should say, "Lord, teach us to pray"—*because we are ignorant in our asking.* Paul said in Romans 8:26, ". . . We know not what we should pray for as we ought . . . ."

As a Christian grows in grace he also experiences a growing consciousness of his inability to pray. Many who are young in the faith have much zeal, a lot of self-confidence, and are not afraid to "rush in where angels fear to tread." They do not hesitate to pray in public–and because they are so young in the faith they think they do "pretty good."

But with maturity comes responsibility, knowledge, and *humility* – and the Christian realizes more and more that to pray a good prayer does not mean "words" that impress an audience, but *heart-felt* words that reach the throne of God. What a great responsibility! To think that a finite being has the right and the privilege of addressing the very throne of God!

If we are willing to be honest we must confess that even at our best in our daily personal prayer life, we are but halting and lame in our praying; and we should be glad for all the help we can get from the Lord in learning how to pray. But this lack of knowledge should not be used as an excuse *not* to pray; it should not cause us to become discouraged to the point of throwing up our hands in defeat. The disciples had been constantly with Jesus, they had heard Him pray many times – yet *they needed to be taught how to pray.*

Some may ask, "What difficulty is there in praying? It requires but a heart to feel, and a tongue to speak our needs. Even an infant can pray." That is all true – but we need help in keeping our heart tuned aright to God, we need guidance in making our tongue speak the right words. This does not require greatness or worldly wisdom, for it is true that the little child can pray. No doubt God hears with acceptance the few jumbled petitions of the infant, when possibly the learned scholar's words of beauty never reach the courts of heaven. The infant asks, with no thought but that God *does* hear and answer.

Prayer without faith is no good (Matt. 17:20). "So

then faith cometh by hearing, and hearing by the Word of God'' (Rom. 10:17). And even if we do not lack in faith, we must admit it is difficult to always know what to pray for. James said, "Ye ask, and receive not, because ye ask amiss . . ." (James 4:3). We are all guilty of selfish praying. We pray sometimes for the right thing—but with the wrong attitude. For instance, many wives only pray for a lost husband to be saved so that their own lives will be made easier. Some pray for their church to grow so that they can boast about it to others. Perhaps a church dispute arises, the church splits, and because of their pride the opposing groups pray for great things to be done—not "for Jesus' sake," but in order that they may boast to the other group. "We will show them!" is their motto. Sometimes, even if we do not pray selfishly, we unknowingly ask for things amiss, and should God grant our request it would not be for our good and His glory.

Because of this, we know that we should pray for God's will to be done when we do not know His will in the matter. This we learned from the model prayer and from other recorded prayers of our Lord. If Jesus the Son prayed, "Thy will be done," how necessary it is for US to do so. We cannot trust our own will, nor always know if our way is correct; but God can see the end from the beginning, while *our* vision is limited to the present. Even if we do not incorporate the words "Thy will be done" into our prayer, our hearts should be surrendered to this fact.

To be able to rest on God's wisdom in the matter of answering our requests is actually a great blessing – but remember, *God can see the heart,* and He knows if you pray "Thy will be done" when you really do not mean it and in truth want your own will at all costs. To many, the phrase "Thy will, not mine, be done" is something to be quoted glibly without really considering what is being said. It is only a form that closes most prayers.

Those who sincerely pray, "Thy will, Lord, instead of mine," should realize the consequences of such a prayer, and also pray for God's grace to *accept* His will.

There are some things which we know are within God's will – for instance, the Word says, "It is not God's will that any should perish, but that all come to repentance." So we know that when we pray for the salvation of the lost, we are praying in His will. Christians or backsliders do not need to pray, "Father, forgive my sins *if it be thy will.*" We know it is God's will to forgive, for I John 1:9 says, "If we confess our sins, He is faithful and just to forgive us our sins, and to cleanse us from all unrighteousness."

As we study God's Word on prayer we can readily see that we need to be taught how to pray and what to pray for. But I repeat: This is no excuse for neglecting prayer. Someone has said that prayer is like Jacob's ladder, connecting earth with heaven (Gen. 28:12), and that there are rounds upon it, adapted to all capacities and conditions. Just because one cannot stand on the topmost round with the mature saints is no reason why he cannot stand on the *bottom round* with the infant! For wherever we stand, we are at least on the ladder and in an attitude of prayer – and we know that God is in an attitude of listening–yes, even to those on the lowest round: "Behold, the Lord's hand is not shortened, that it cannot save; *neither His ear heavy, that it cannot hear*" (Isa. 59:1).

II.

"Lord, teach us to pray" – *because of a sense of our own sinfulness.* We often hear someone say (and perhaps we ourselves have said), "That person has a gift of prayer." More times than not, we arrive at that conclusion because the person has a beautiful vocabulary and speaks with fluency. Yet we know from sad experience that some of the most beautiful prayers have been uttered by men whom we later found to be wicked and sinful. They had a "gift of *words*," but not of prayer.

For example, when the Pharisee and the publican went up to the temple to pray, the Pharisee knew how to use words and make an impressive prayer, but the poor publican could only say, "*Lord, be merciful to me, a sinner.*" Yet *he* went home justified while the Pharisee went home with sins unforgiven. Outward expression, however beautiful, does not necessarily indicate a "gift of prayer."

Insofar as I can find, it is not scriptural to use the term "*gift*" *of prayer.* We read of the gift of teaching, the gift of prophecy, and various other gifts (I Cor. 12:1–11; Eph. 4:11), but prayer is not listed among them. In Zechariah 12:10 we read, "I will pour upon the house of David, and upon the inhabitants of Jerusalem, *the spirit of grace and of supplications.*" The Holy Spirit indwells every child of God; therefore, if you are born again you are as capable of praying as is any other Christian.

Praying a good prayer depends upon the spirit to pray aright. A petition, though uttered in broken sentences and stumbling phrases, if prayed from a heart that is right with God is truly a good prayer.

In Psalm 66:18 we read, "If I regard iniquity in my heart, the Lord will not hear me." This verse of Scripture rather confounds me. It seems that so much of answered prayer depends on the truth of this passage. In Isaiah 53:5 we read, "He was wounded for our transgressions, He was bruised for our iniquities . . . ." I looked up the word "iniquities" in the New Testament dictionary and found that it means *lawlessness and unrighteousness.*

In Romans 6:18 Paul tells us that when we become free from sin we become the servants of righteousness, and in verse 19 of the same chapter he says that as previously we yielded "to iniquity unto iniquity," we are now to yield our members as servants of "righteousness unto holiness."

This seems to point to the fact that when one is saved, iniquity, in its essential meaning, is removed. Therefore, one who regards (looks upon with favor) iniquity in the heart must not be saved. Jesus Christ came to bear the iniquity of the sinner, and it seems to me that one who is truly *saved* has the righteousness of God in Jesus Christ and therefore cannot regard iniquity in his heart, nor look upon unrighteousness with favor.

In John 9:31 we read, "*Now we know that God heareth not sinners.*" The quotation from Psalm 66 could mean the same. If so, then it refers to the iniquity and unrighteousness that Jesus puts under the blood when we accept Him as Saviour.

On the other hand, if this verse does apply to Christians and is a condition to prayer being heard by God, then we must interpret it to mean *sins*, as in I John 1:9, and not the initial iniquity (sin) which was changed to God's righteousness at the new birth. Jesus came "to take away the SIN of the world." It is the *sin* (singular) of unbelief that damns the soul, not the *fruit* of unbelief which we classify as *sins* (plural).

Because Christians are still in the flesh, we commit *sins.* It is impossible to live a sinless perfect life in this tabernacle of flesh, even though we do have a new heart. I do not mean that Christians commit the sins most people *catalog* as sins—such as drinking, cursing, cheating, lying, etc.; but Christians cannot live a *sinless* life even though they do not do any of the things the world counts as sin. James said, "*To him that knoweth to do good, and doeth it not, to him it is sin*"! And Luke 17:10 tells us, "When ye shall have done all those things which are commanded you, say, We are unprofitable servants: we have done that which was our duty to do."

The First Epistle of John was written to Christians. John says, "My little children," and then tells us that the epistle was written *that our joy might be full.* In I John 1:9 we are told that "If we confess our sins, He is faithful and just to forgive us our sins, and to cleanse us from all unrighteousness." The Christian who has unconfessed sins in the heart *cannot have joy.*

Through many years of work in revival meetings and close association with those in the prayer room, I find that Christians who have truly backslidden and who carry unconfessed sins in the heart soon stop praying. They *cannot* pray because their guilty conscience holds up the sin in their lives and they cannot approach God without first confessing or acknowledging that sin. When a backslider starts to pray, his cry is "Lord, *forgive my sins*!" In other words, a true backslider stops all semblance of praying until, with a broken and contrite heart, he confesses his sins.

Jonah is an example of this. God told Jonah to preach to the people of Nineveh; Jonah rebelled and fled "from the presence of the Lord." Next we find him, disobedient and backslidden, boarding a ship to Tarshish. But although Jonah was fleeing from God's presence, God kept His eye on him. After the ship was under way, "the Lord sent out a great wind into the sea," and a great storm arose. The mariners were afraid "and cried every man unto his god."

However, we do not find *Jonah* praying, but *sleeping* down in the ship. He could not pray for deliverance from the storm until he had experienced a change of heart toward God's command. If he *had* prayed to God for deliverance from the storm, that prayer, I believe, would have been recorded in the Bible. Jonah did no praying until after he had been thrown overboard, according to the second chapter of the book of Jonah. It is recorded in verses one and two of that chapter, "Then Jonah prayed unto the Lord his God . . . and said, I cried *by reason of mine affliction unto the Lord*, and He heard me . . . ." In the last of his prayer he said, "*I will pay that that I have vowed*" (verse 9). He had experienced a change of heart, and it was then—and only then—that the Lord delivered him upon dry ground.

Only a sinner or a hypocrite recites prayers *without repentance*. A true backslider will be convicted of his backsliding, and God will make him miserable. "Whom the Lord loveth, He chasteneth . . ." (Heb. 12:6).

If the verse in Psalm 66 is applicable to Christians, we can readily see that God will not hear His child who is living in sin until that child asks forgiveness. There may be many Christians who, though not backsliders and not living in sin, have some "thorn in the flesh"—and yet they try to carry on their prayer life and ignore their spiritual failures.

These must be the most miserable of all people! Surely they must know that God can see every thought, every hidden thing, in the heart. Yet they are afraid to bring it out in the open, confess it to God, and ask for help; so they fool themselves into trying to ignore it, leaving the subject out of their prayers—and they end up by being wretched, doubtful, and with no assurance as to whether God hears them or not.

Even the most devout Christians, those who do not try to hide things from God, have a sense of unworthiness and sinfulness as they approach the throne of God's holiness – and because of this feeling of unworthiness many say, "I cannot pray. There is no use to pray; God will not hear me." But that is the wrong attitude to take. If there are no known sins in your life and you are walking in all the light God has given you, you are as much a prayer warrior as the best saint you know. After all, we are all finite beings. We who are saved are all children of God, and if we pray in the right spirit we can have as much power in prayer as others.

Let us consider *the right spirit* concerning prayer. Are our prayers offered in humility? Are they sincere, fervent prayers from a heart of faith? Or do we pray with divided thoughts, pretending to pray while our minds wander in a dozen different directions? Who does not wonder at times why God does not cut us down in anger at such times? (I feel sure He *would*, if we did not have a High Priest who can be touched with the feeling of our infirmities, who was in all points tempted as we are, yet was without sin – Heb. 4:15.)

With all of our human weaknesses, how we do need to be taught of God to restrain our wandering thoughts and fix our whole soul in sweet and full communion with Him! Can you think of many things in this world that are more desirable than the perfect spirit of prayer? I cannot. How my soul cries out to God to teach me so to pray that I will know that I have been in direct contact with Him, feel His presence, and know that what I ask in His name will be given!

"And this is the confidence that we have in Him,

that, if we ask any thing according to His will, He heareth us" (I John 5:14).

"And whatsoever ye shall ask in my name, that will I do, that the Father may be glorified in the Son" (John 14:13).

"And I say unto you, Ask, and it shall be given you; seek, and ye shall find; knock, and it shall be opened unto you" (Luke 11:9).

"And all things, whatsoever ye shall ask in prayer, believing, ye shall receive" (Matt. 21:22).

III.

"Lord, teach us to pray"—*that we may be consistent and persevering in our prayers.* If every petition we offered were granted, we would have many things which we do not want, and things would happen which we would eventually see were not for our good. We cannot quote too often "Ye ask, and receive not, because ye ask amiss."

This is a truth which none of us can deny, but even with the human tendency to "ask amiss" we should never cease to be consistent in prayer. Not all of our prayers are amiss—especially the prayers of those who are sincerely trying to pray in God's will. Certainly we would enjoy more abundant blessings if we were more consistent in prayer. Shall we have the bitter thought that if we had been more faithful in our prayer life, our loved one, friend, or neighbor might not have died without giving us any hope that he was saved?

Suppose we knew that the soul of a friend depended entirely upon our intercession for him. Would we be more faithful in prayer? Someone's eternal destiny may depend upon us; we should never forget that. Prayer *does* avail for others—and if we value the life and soul of our loved ones who are unsaved, let us ask sincerely, "Lord, teach us how to be *faithful* in prayer!" And let us not be content to offer the same formal prayer for these lost ones year after year; but rather, let us fervently, earnestly plead for their souls until we get the answer to our prayers.

In Mark 7:24–30 we find a marvelous example of perseverance. A Syrophenician woman came to Jesus and asked Him to heal her daughter. He said to her, "Let the children first be filled: for it is not meet to take the children's bread, and to cast it unto the dogs." But that discouraging reply did not stop this sincere woman; she would not take "No" for an answer. She continued asking until Jesus answered her prayer.

The majority of Christians are guilty of asking God for something, and then because we meet with the discouragement of what we deem to be *unanswered* prayer we give up in defeat, saying, "It was not God's will to answer me." It was called to my attention some time ago by a friend of mine that at the end of a prayer many people use the expression, "If it can be thy will" without thought and more as a habit than for any other reason – and then they say, "It must not be God's will" as an excuse for unanswered prayer, when actually the unanswered prayer is due to lack of faith.

I am sure this is true. For example, when we leave home to go to a meeting (or anywhere else, for that matter) we pray for God to keep us from harm and see us safely to our destination. If we close our prayer for a safe journey by saying, "If it can be thy will," it may be that we, because of our human weakness, do so in order to leave a loophole–just in case we have a wreck. On the other hand, I believe that in the majority of cases we honestly mean to completely commit ourselves into God's hands. When we do this, we conscientiously trust Him to see us safely through–and any by-product of the trip, any inconvenience, we accept as His will, still having utmost faith in His ability to take care of us.

This is certainly something to think about. It challenges our purpose and sincerity when we pray, "Thy will be done."

There have been other times – serious times – in our lives, when we did not know God's will. We knew what we wanted – but try as we would, we could not know the mind of God concerning the situation. *Then* we became willing for God to act, for His will to be done – and never has He disappointed us!

The Syrophenician woman did not ask Jesus to cast the demons out of her daughter *if it were His will to do so*– for He came into the world "to seek and to save that which was lost." When she ran into unanswered prayer, she humbled herself still more. She said, "Yes, Lord–yet the dogs under the table eat of the children's crumbs!" Jesus answered by making her daughter whole.

Oh, how I pray for patience, for the will and the ability to persevere in prayer! Weakness of spirit, lack of faith – these cause us to give up. May we be like the man in Luke 11:5–10 who kept knocking until he was given the bread he asked for.

And who can so well teach us to pray as the Lord Jesus Christ? He is our Intercessor in heaven: ". . . And if any man sin, we have an Advocate with the Father, Jesus Christ the righteous" (I John 2:1).

He is our Mediator between God and man. He knows what pleas will prevail with God, and He can put them into our hearts and order them aright upon our tongues.

"Likewise the Spirit also helpeth our infirmities: for we know not what we should pray for as we ought: but the Spirit itself maketh intercession for us with groanings which cannot be uttered. And He that searcheth the hearts knoweth what is the mind of the Spirit, because He maketh intercession for the saints according to the will of God" (Rom. 8:26,27).

Do not be deceived into thinking that there is a great secret or mystery to praying which can be known by only a few. But it is true that all the passages on prayer in the Bible point to the fact that there is a greater privilege in prayer than the average Christian enjoys—not because he *cannot*, but because he *will* not avail himself of this comfort and nearness of access to God which he could enjoy.

A Christian who is *right* in his *heart* and who fervently, consistently goes to God in prayer, will enjoy answered prayer and manifold blessings in his devotional life.

"Seeing then that we have a great high priest, that is passed into the heavens, Jesus the Son of God, let us hold fast our profession. For we have not an high priest which cannot be touched with the feeling of our infirmities; but was in all points tempted like as we are, yet without sin. Let us therefore come boldly unto the throne of grace, that we may obtain mercy, and find grace to help in time of need" (Heb. 4:14–16).

Where to pray? Is it necessary to go to a certain place to pray? I think the Bible is clear on this point. We have the admonition to "pray without ceasing"—*pray everywhere.* Read Acts 6:4; I Thessalonians 5:17; I Timothy 2:8.

In the sixth chapter of Matthew Jesus rebuked the Pharisees for standing on the street corners and praying to be heard of men. He then says, in *contrast* to their actions, that we are to go into the closet, shut the door, and pray.

I do not believe that Jesus is here teaching that we can pray only in a closet. He is pointing out the truth that when one prays to be heard of men, he has not been heard by God. Real and sincere prayer is not done to impress people, but for God's ears only. True, there is a time to go into a prayer closet, close the door, and stay there until the burden is lifted; but much praying—and *real* praying—is done by Christians anywhere and everywhere, and yet their fellowman knows not of it.

But how are we to know when to go into the closet to pray? Here again I believe that is taught us by the Lord. The Holy Spirit in the heart leads the child of God: "For as many as are led by the Spirit of God, they are the sons of God" (Rom. 8:14). A person who is right with God will have a definite desire or burden to steal away and pray.

The Bible mentions a *place* of prayer (Acts 16:13); "the *house* of prayer" (Matt. 21:13); and "the *hour* of prayer" (Acts 3:1). We can pray anywhere, any time; but there are certain places more adapted to prayer than others are, and we should have a certain time for special devotions.

If we were to argue the technicality of prayer, we might come to the conclusion that praying is far too difficult to understand; but if we think back over the Scriptures on prayer, we can see that God has left the door wide open and even the most untaught child of God can walk into the holy of holies in prayer! Any Christian who is right with God can pray anywhere, at any time. It is not words of wisdom that reach heaven, but the prayer of *faith*, offered in humility.

And remember—*prayer changes things*. The weakest, smallest, most insignificant Christian has at his disposal the weapon to remove mountains of troubles and change the course of rivers of opposition in his life, in the life of his family, or in the church!

Prayer is our privilege – therefore let us pray for God to teach us through His Word and the leadership of the Holy Spirit *HOW to pray.*

NUMBERING OUR DAYS

NUMBERING OUR DAYS

"So teach us to number our days, that we may apply our hearts unto wisdom" (Psalm 90:12).

In this brief prayer, what days and what kind of numbering was the Psalmist referring to? Did he refer to days that were *past*? Surely he could count *them*; he knew his age, and he did not need to call upon God to help him to number days past.

Did he refer to days yet *future*? If so, how could he expect to number *them*—for no one can know the number of days he has left to live.

Please notice the wording of the prayer: ". . . *Teach* us to number . . . ." A man of David's age and ability most surely had been taught *how to count* when he was young. Simple reasoning leads us to believe that he was praying to be taught to number his days in a sense very different from the mere use of arithmetic in estimating how many days there had been—or would be—in his life. This numbering of which he speaks requires a higher counting and cannot be accomplished without help from God.

I understand this prayer as if the Psalmist said, "Teach me to *meditate* upon the days that are past, and to become deeply impressed with the time I have wasted and lost; and when I think of the *future*, help me to be ever mindful of the need for diligence and faithfulness in improving the time yet to come. Oh, God! Help me as your steward, as one who will soon be called into judgment, to apply myself to the only true wisdom—that of *service to God*!"

To "apply our hearts unto wisdom" we must first

apply our hearts unto God in earnest supplication. We need God's help in taking the right view of days past and gone, with their lessons in humility, repentance, warning, chastisement, thankfulness, and faith. We need wisdom from above in order to rightly contemplate the future—for all that we know of our days from now to the grave is that *the time is short*, however many days are numbered on the calendar of time. We should attempt with God's help to number our days by comparing the past in connection with the life to come, that we may not sleep as some do, but that we may be alert, redeeming the time, working while it is still *today*.

Let us begin with the days that are past. How shall we attempt to number them—*by trying to account for them*? What standard of measurement shall we use? The most important thing known to God or man is the salvation of the soul and our relationship to God. Let us take that and use it as our yardstick:

Days should not be called "days of life" if those days have been spent in the service of the devil. "She that liveth in pleasure is dead while she liveth" (I Tim. 5:6). Everyone who has not been saved is *spiritually dead*; the man who has just *been saved* has already lived longer than all his previous years, for now he is truly "alive unto God." There is a vast difference between those who are alive unto God and those who are not.

There is also a marked contrast in the manner of life among God's children, some of whom seem to be barely alive (the most you can say for them is that they are not spiritually dead), while others are vigorously enjoying the Christian experience. Some Christians who have spiritual life within them, have so poorly nourished that life from the Word of God and by faithful prayer that there is no vigor nor zealous enjoyment of spiritual blessings. In such a life, fruit is scanty, yielding only enough to prove that the tree is not dead. Such Christians are indifferent to God's work around them; they attend church–but they have no zeal to take others with them. Because there IS life within them, they are occasionally stirred and their enthusiasm is noticed briefly; but when revival fire burns down they lapse once more into a coma of indifference. It seems incredible that a truly saved person could BE so indifferent as to give the appearance of not caring if others go to hell. Undoubtedly, such a one is also indifferent to his own lukewarm condition.

Indifferent Christians need to awaken to the fact that they are *sleeping on the job.* One of these days the chastening hand of God will fall heavily upon them. Should they suddenly go out to meet Him, they would be ashamed to face their blessed Saviour!

In other Christians there is life, vigor, and spiritual alertness. They have a heart for prayer, a heart of love, zeal, labor, joy, and peace. They feed upon the Word; they constantly grow in grace and are faithful in bringing others to a knowledge of their Saviour and Lord. In the life of such Christians, every day adds to its numbering, no days are completely blank, and a *year* in such a life is longer and adds up to more treasure in heaven than does an entire *lifetime* of a lukewarm, undecided, half-worldly, uninspiring life with which so many Christians are content.

It is my desire to cause you to stop and reflect upon the past and measure your past according to Bible numbering. Christian, of what value is all the time you spent before you really began to live? Some of you can recall days of worldliness, of ingratitude and disobedience–and even days of shame. However the days of our past were spent, I am sure none of us can recall them without giving thanks in our heart that God spared us until such time as we were saved; *but taking account from the time you were saved,* what do your days as a child of God amount to? How much time have you wasted? What have you done for Christ? How much have you grown in grace?

For the most of us, an honest viewing of the past puts us to shame. Such reflection should humble our souls – and while we look at ourselves in humiliation, we must *look up* for consolation. Only through the mercy of God and the intercession of the Lord Jesus Christ can we find help . . . certainly it is not to be found in our own strength and merit.

Those who have *not* been born again comprise another group who should number their days. Sinner friend, how long have you lived? Most of you will have to admit that you have lived long enough and had opportunities enough to become a child of God–and long enough to heap up a fearful account of convictions ignored!

But there is another confession, if you will be honest and truthful with yourself: Has not all of your life been one of sin and rebellion against God? The question is asked in love, and I hope you will accept it in the spirit in which it is asked, sincerely considering it, that the present numbering of your days may be as God will number them at the judgment. One day you will have to give an account, and at that time it will be too late to do anything about it.

Usually a person brought face to face with the question of the past and of his soul's salvation begins to make excuses by counting his good points, thus proving that he is not such a "lost" person, after all. It may be true that you have done many good deeds—perhaps even more than many professing Christians; but if you have neglected *the one essential thing* the Lord demands of you, all other deeds count for nothing in His sight.

An example of this is found in the parable in Luke 13:6–9: "A certain man had a fig tree planted in his vineyard . . . ." The fact that the fig tree was PLANTED proves that there was a purpose in its being where it was . . . it was in a *vineyard*, in cultivated, fertilized ground—not by the side of the road nor on a rocky hillside by chance.

The Bible tells us that the owner of the vineyard "came and sought fruit thereon, and found none." Thus we see that the purpose for the planting of the tree was *that it might provide fruit.* The tree had every opportunity to produce fruit, yet it bore nothing but leaves. Not even one tiny, shriveled fig was to be found upon it!

YOU have been "planted" in a country where the Gospel is preached. The means of grace enriches the vineyard in which you live, and the water of the river of God's love flows through it. Yet you, knowing full well what God expects of you, refuse to comply with His command, "Ye must be born again."

The Bible further says of the fig tree, "Then said (the owner) to the dresser of his vineyard, These three years have I come seeking fruit of this fig tree, and found none. Cut it down! Why cumbereth it the ground?"

Did the fig tree deserve such a hard saying? True, it had never produced a fig—but it HAD produced *an abundance of leaves.* It had not been entirely useless, for the birds of the air found a home in its branches, and weary laborers found rest under the shade of its foliage. Its falling leaves also helped to enrich the soil—but the tree failed to do the one thing required of it: *It did not bear fruit.*

Is that not like YOU when you plead that though you have not been saved you *have* done a lot for the church and for humanity? What you need to see is that the question is not "What good have you done?" but "*Where is your heart and what have you done with Jesus Christ?*" You may prove that you have not lived in vain–but *have you lived unto God*? The voice of God has followed you at every step, pleading "Give me your heart"–but never has that voice been obeyed. Instead, you have offered nothing but leaves – and as sure as the barren fig tree was condemned, so must your days be numbered as living in sin and rebellion against God, even though you may have given a fortune, time, and talent in doing good deeds for others.

This is a fearful view of the past, especially since you do not know how short the future may be before you go into eternity. What about that future? How long have you yet to live? How many days have you yet to number before you go out into that life that has no days, no years, no end of centuries–a life that will go on *forever and ever*! To be able to say, "I have ten days . . . two weeks . . . ten years," is impossible. That kind of numbering is in God's hands; but by God's yardstick we can measure our future to some extent, and see how short a life we have and how precious is our time.

"One day is with the Lord as a thousand years, and a thousand years as one day." *God's* measure of duration is *eternity*, and according to that measure, man's life–even the longest life–is very short. James 4:14 sets forth a good illustration of the brevity of life on earth:

"Whereas ye know not what shall be on the morrow.

For what is your life? It is even a *vapour*, that appeareth for a little time, and then *vanisheth away*." In the light of eternity, the LONGEST life is as a vapor that appears for a moment and then vanishes into nothingness.

From childhood, how far away seems the age of seventy–our allotted three score and ten years; but from wherever we stand now, *how short* the years appear as we look back to childhood; and from a deathbed our years on this earth will seem very short indeed. With what soberness and sincerity of heart you should view these days that will determine where you will spend eternity! For when you come down to death's door and the Great Beyond opens before you, the most important thing to you then will be whether or not you have been born again.

We speak of dying–but *shall* we ever die? If Jesus tarries, these *bodies* will die; but WE (the soul within that thinks, sees, speaks, feels, remembers, enjoys, and suffers) will *never* die. The soul could not die, if it *would*; once embarked in life it must go on and on forever. There is no door through which we can escape out of being, and even after this life we will live forever–in one place or another–heaven or hell; the choice is ours.

In our present bodies, and with our finite minds having such limited knowledge, it is difficult to grasp the truth of life that will go on and on through limitless ages to come; but if we cannot *compute*, at least we can *contemplate*. We cannot measure the ocean, but we can look upon it and compare its greatness in contrast to the narrow streams that pour into it. In like manner, we can consider the shortness of our days as compared with the thought of an endless forever. Such sincere consideration should enable us to answer the question of our Lord which remains unanswered by many: "What shall it profit a man if he shall gain the whole world–and lose his own soul?" (Mark 8:36). If we would but think on eternity, we could obtain a proper perspective of the preciousness of the hope we have in the salvation of our Lord Jesus Christ, and the incomparable smallness of everything else in contrast!

"That we may apply our hearts unto wisdom." What IS wisdom? Sinner friend, only ONE thing is wisdom for YOU, and all else is foolishness. *It is wisdom for you to accept Jesus Christ as your Saviour.* I intreat you, for the sake of your poor soul so long neglected; in the name of the God whose peace is so precious but whose wrath is a consuming fire; in the name of Jesus, the most gracious Saviour, whose love and suffering you have so ungratefully slighted; delay no more – accept Christ as your Saviour now!

Christian friend, what is the wisdom to which *your* heart should be applied? I answer: *the wisdom of a greater earnestness in the work and life becoming to a child of God.* At best you have but a short time to live for the glory of your God in this world. You have but a short time in which to win the souls of those about you who are lost and on their way to a devil's hell. To live and pray and work as you know you should, will insure that you will fear neither death nor the judgment. Such wisdom comes only from God, and we must pray to be taught of Him, to make our days count for Him and for His glory (James 1:5).

THE DEAD IN CHRIST

THE DEAD IN CHRIST

"And I heard a voice from heaven saying unto me, Write, Blessed are the dead which die in the Lord from henceforth: Yea, saith the Spirit, that they may rest from their labours; and their works do follow them" (Rev. 14:13).

The dead! Where *are* they? More specifically, *where are the dead IN CHRIST*? One thing we know: They are where we who are saved are soon to go.

This Scripture is speaking of the dead as they are NOW, *before the resurrection*—not as they will be *after* the resurrection. (They will *then* have a glorified body, alive not only in spirit, but in body as well; and they will be *alive forevermore*—in power and perfection of life altogether new.) But it is of the present state of the dead in Christ that our Scripture speaks—those whose earthly tabernacle is dissolved. They are "absent from the body, but present with the Lord." They have passed from earth and from our sight, but not one of them has passed out of life (existence).

There are two classifications of people who have passed into eternity: The *saved*, and the *lost*. Neither have passed "out of life." What a multitude the past generations have poured into that great eternity! But one eternal fact remains: They are ALL found on one side or the other of that great line of separation, the only distinction among us who are living that will remain when we, too, pass on into eternity. Rich or poor, bond or free, cultured or illiterate, small or great, *those* distinctions vanish when we are laid in the grave.

There is one distinction, however, that lasts forever.

It runs its line among those who have departed this life, the same as it now divides those in the land of the living. This distinction separates us into two categories–those who are IN Christ, and those who are OUT of Christ. In our Scripture text in Revelation we are told of the present state of those who died IN CHRIST JESUS.

What Does It Mean to "Die in the Lord"?

It is the last act on earth of *being* in the Lord – for it is a settled fact that every born again Christian is NOW *in Christ*:

"There is therefore now no condemnation to them which are IN Christ Jesus, who walk not after the flesh, but after the Spirit" (Rom. 8:1). Therefore, when death comes for us, it finds us exactly *where we lived* – "in the Lord." To die in the Lord is not getting into some new shelter, nor putting on some new armor. It is not the coming into a new relationship with Christ. From the moment we are saved, our lives are "hid with Christ in God" (Col. 3:3), and to *die* in the Lord is just a continuation of a relationship formed when our Christian life began; it is just the abiding of the soul in the Ark which it entered when Christ was received.

To die in the Lord is simply for the Christian to pass through the valley and the shadow of death precisely as he passed through the dangers, temptations, trials, sorrows, and duties of this mortal life where God has promised, "My grace is sufficient for thee: for my strength is made perfect in weakness" (II Cor. 12:9). ". . . For He hath said, I will never leave thee, nor forsake thee. So that we may boldly say, The Lord is my helper, and I will not fear what man shall do unto me" (Heb. 13:5,6).

To die in the Lord is *faith overcoming in the last conflict* exactly as it has done in all previous conflicts of the Christian life—the same faith, resting on the same promises, passing through Jordan as the Israelites passed the Red Sea—always, yea, *always* "looking unto Jesus."

To die in Christ is for the child of God to fall asleep in the same arms of redeeming love in which he was embraced at the time of his salvation and where he was always safe in the peace of God. "The eternal God is thy refuge, and underneath are the everlasting arms" (Deut. 33:27).

But these things apply *only to those who are IN CHRIST.* Those who are OUT of Christ have no hope, none of these consolations. Once IN Christ, we are in possession of all that belongs to the preciousness of the Gospel. Condemnation is no more; there is grace sufficient for us to live by and grace abundant for us to die by. We have an inheritance incorruptible, reserved in heaven for us (I Pet. 1:4). All of this we have IN CHRIST—and all because we ARE in Him! The great question before you, then, is "Are you IN Christ–NOW?" Is Christ your righteousness?

What does it mean to be IN CHRIST NOW? We are in Him when, being united to Him by receiving His Spirit and His sacrificial death for our sins, *His righteousness is imputed to us.* That is GOD'S part. On *our* part, that which unites us to Christ is our faith: "For what saith the Scripture? Abraham *believed God,* and it was counted unto him for righteousness" (Rom. 4:3).

The life which the Christian lives in the flesh is a life of faith. Paul said, "I am crucified with Christ: nevertheless I live; yet not I, but Christ liveth in me: and the life which I now live in the flesh *I live by the faith of the Son of God,* who loved me, and gave Himself for me" (Gal. 2:20).

The Christian life, from beginning to end–in all of its hopes, its works, its growth, its conflicts and final victory–is simply a life of faith, derived from Christ. Jesus is "the author and finisher of our faith" (Heb. 12:2). On our part, nothing else makes us to be IN CHRIST. The moment we put our faith in Him as Saviour we are IN Him, and our continuance in Him is simply the continued exercising of that same faith.

The Christian's progress (or growth) in Christ is the increase of the strength of that same faith through the Word: "As newborn babes, desire the sincere milk of the Word, that ye may grow thereby" (I Pet. 2:2).

In the wonderful eleventh chapter of Hebrews, Paul lists the patriarchs who were examples of faith: "By faith *Abel* offered unto God a more excellent sacrifice than Cain . . . ." By faith Enoch . . . Noah . . . Abraham . . . Isaac . . . Jacob (and others) lived, labored, suffered–and having *lived by faith*, the Scripture tells us that they also *DIED in faith*!

I know of no better illustration of the connection between a Christian's life and a Christian's death. *Where faith LED them, death FOUND them*–resting on the everlasting arms of Jesus, ready to do their duty right where they were. The promises that sustained them through the trials of life were their great consolation in the conflict of death.

There is another place where Paul speaks of being *in the Lord* that is so striking I must mention it here:

In Philippians 3:8,9 he says, ". . . I count all things but loss for the excellency of the knowledge of Christ Jesus my Lord: for whom I have suffered the loss of all things, and do count them but dung, that I may win Christ, *and be found in Him . . . .*"

To be "FOUND IN HIM." Here is precisely what I am talking about. To die in the Lord is, at death, to be found in Him. Paul counted all things as utterly worthless compared to this. Does he tell us what it *means* to be found "in Him"? Yes, he does—in the very next words:

"*. . . Not having mine own righteousness, which is of the law, but that which is through the faith of Christ, the righteousness which is of God by faith*!" In these words we see two kinds of righteousness:

1. *Our own righteousness*—our own works and merits; a righteousness which will avail us nothing at the time of death: ". . . We are all as an unclean thing, and all our righteousnesses are as filthy rags . . ." (Isa. 64:6).

"Not by works of righteousness which we have done, but according to His mercy He saved us, by the washing of regeneration, and renewing of the Holy Ghost" (Titus 3:5).

2. *A righteousness which is through the faith of Christ*—the righteousness which is of God by faith. Not the righteousness of the sinner, but that of the sinner's *Saviour* who fulfilled the law, satisfied every demand of God, and is thereby able to save to the uttermost all who will come unto God by Him.

These definitions and descriptions of righteousness are so far apart it is difficult to see how even those who have heard the Gospel but a few times could confuse them! We cannot wear them both; it is impossible to trust in our *own* righteousness and that of the Saviour at the same time.

It is alarming to find *anyone* (at any age) who is counting on his faithfulness to the church to get him into heaven – but to me the most heartbreaking experience of all is to find a precious lady or gentleman who has reached a ripe old age and will soon be passing on from this life, who is trusting in a good life (self-righteousness) to get them into the kingdom of God! What is even more touching is that most of these dear old people are moral, humble, sincere, so very precious—and yet *so deceived*! (As a rule, a self-righteous person is arrogant, conceited, and self-satisfied.)

Only recently I spoke with a lady who was past sixty years of age. She was sweet and gracious to me in her answers to my questions, but when I asked her, "*Do you know that you are saved*?" she replied, "I HOPE so. I do not know of anything I do that is wrong. I have been trying to live for Jesus for more than fifty years – I joined the church when I was just a girl."

What can one do to arouse such a sweet, gentle character from her state of deception? She actually believed that she would be guilty of *boasting* if she said, "I KNOW that I am saved." To a great extent I blame the pastors for such a state of spiritual ignorance. This lady should have been taught that our salvation is *God's* righteousness, and that it depends upon HIS faithfulness—not upon our righteousness nor our faithfulness.

To acknowledge assurance of salvation is not bragging on *self* but on *the Christ who died so that we could be saved*! When we accept the righteousness of Christ we will then be found in Him—sheltered as perfectly from the condemnation of sin as Noah in the ark was sheltered from the waters of the flood. Beloved, if you live in Christ, have no fear! When death comes it will find you where you lived—*in Christ Jesus*!

The Blessedness of Those Who Die in the Lord

Is this some new truth just revealed to John—a truth withheld from the other saints? I think not, for many years before John penned The Revelation, Paul had said, ". . . Whilst we are at home in the body, we are absent from the Lord . . . and willing rather to be absent from the body, and to be present with the Lord" (II Cor. 5:6,8).

First, let us see *where*, in Revelation, this plain and familiar truth is recorded: *It is found in the midst of the prophecies concerning the persecutions of the saints by Antichrist*, and these prophecies have to do with a definite time–the Tribulation period after the Church is raptured out of this world.

John foretells "things that will be hereafter," and in the midst of the record of the terrible persecution of God's people he abruptly declares, "Here is the patience of the saints: here are they that keep the commandments of God, and the faith of Jesus" (Rev. 14:12). Then to comfort them in their struggle comes the declaration, "I heard a voice from heaven saying unto me, Write, *Blessed are the dead which die in the Lord from henceforth*."

Mark the word "*henceforth*." Does this mean *from the time John wrote these words*? Or does it refer to *a time in the distant future*, as if the voice from heaven were saying that the dead would be blessed "henceforth" from the time in the Tribulation period when the cry went out that Babylon had fallen, and the doom of the beast worshippers was announced? (Rev. 14:8–11).

Such an interpretation would mean that it was given only to the Tribulation saints to be blessed and to rest from their labors. It would mean that the distinction of the state of the dead depended on *times and external events* in this life, and not on the *inward state* of the believer. It would mean that the saints are blessed–not *because they die in the Lord*–but because they die at a certain period, amidst certain events!

This could not possibly be true because it would be in direct contradiction to other Scriptures. Paul, in speaking of the departed saints in general, teaches that to die *IN Christ* is to be *WITH Christ* (II Cor. 5:8,9; Phil. 1:23) and therefore blessed, because to be in the presence of Christ is to partake of the most glorious rest. To be *present* with Christ does not mean soul-sleep, but rather, *alive and with HIM.*

There is no time passage between death and being present with the Lord. In Revelation 7 John gives the record of the great multitude saved out of "great tribulation" (verse 14). They were before the throne – and please notice that the fact of their being before the throne, blessed and glorified, did not rest upon their coming out of great tribulation, but upon their wearing the righteousness of Christ. They had "washed their robes, and made them white in the blood of the Lamb." In other words, they had died "*in the Lord.*"

Please notice that John records this passage concerning a group of saints who were before the throne of God, *blessed and resting*, BEFORE he heard the voice from heaven saying, "Blessed are the dead which die in the Lord from henceforth."

Comparing Scripture with Scripture, we must then interpret the "henceforth" to mean, "Blessed are the dead in Christ *from the time of their DYING*"–as if it were written, "Blessed *from the moment of death* are those who die in the Lord." This interpretation would be in harmony with the teaching of Jesus in Luke 16:22, with the stoning of Stephen in Acts 7:54–60, and with the teaching of Paul in II Corinthians 5:8 and Philippians 1:20–23, which were written *before* John was given his revelation on the isle of Patmos. Viewed in this light, it was very appropriate that John might hear a voice from heaven declaring *anew* so precious a truth, in the midst of a prophecy of horrible persecution!

Today we need to refresh the memory and teach this marvelous truth as never before. A truth so dear to believers when dying, should not be kept hidden–concealed by the rubbish of false doctrine and vain traditions. The deadly doctrine of "soul-sleep" is sweeping across our country – and fundamental preachers act as though they were embarrassed to expose these false teachers! I realize that a great many preachers are of modern thought and do not believe the fundamental truths of the Bible; but in this hour of darkness when approximately fifty percent of the religious people believe in soul-sleep, there is great need of a revival of the doctrine of the *present blessedness of the dead in Christ* from the very moment of death.

Thousands of church members (and many *Christians*) know little or nothing about life after death. To know this precious truth will cast out fear and bring comfort to those who are nearing death's door, for they that die in the Lord are blessed in death itself. To those who are found in Christ, the sting of death is taken away, the terror of death is gone. "Precious in the sight of the Lord is the death of His saints" (Psalm 116:15).

It is blessed to know that in death we can commit ourselves wholly to Him as never before. We can say with confidence and a peace sweeter than ever realized before, "The Lord is my Shepherd, I shall not want. . . I shall fear no evil, for thou art with me!"

The dead in Christ are blessed (happy) in being with the Lord. They rest from their labors, "*and their works do follow them.*" Mark this well: *The works FOLLOW*– they do not *precede* the saints to open the door of heaven!

JESUS goes *before.*

Salvation is "not of works, lest any man should boast" (Eph. 2:9). The door is Jesus, and through our faith IN Him we are allowed to enter THROUGH Him. Because of the grace of God, the believer's *works* are accepted, feeble though they may be; and those works continue to follow him because the work done here on earth lives on and produces *more* works. At the judgment seat of Christ the believers will be rewarded for their works, and their reward will be *according* to their works.

May we now make sure that we abide in Christ and He in us, so that when we come down to the chambers of death we will have the comforting assurance, "Blessed are ye that die in the Lord, for ye shall rest from your labors."

WHAT DOES IT MEAN TO BELIEVE ON THE LORD JESUS CHRIST?

WHAT DOES IT MEAN TO BELIEVE ON THE LORD JESUS CHRIST?

The Bible teaches, "*Believe on the Lord Jesus Christ, and thou shalt be saved.*" But how does one believe on Jesus? How can we know when we have believed on Him? To many, "believing" was easy – but to countless thousands the words "believe" and "faith" are mysteries hard to understand.

They say, "I have always believed in Jesus. I have always believed the Bible; yet I do not know whether or not I am saved." That little word "faith" stops them – yet it is faith that makes salvation so simple and so easy man has a hard time accepting it. The devil has blinded the eyes of mankind to the simplicity of salvation (II Cor. 4:4), and put it into the human heart that man must DO something in order to be saved. "Faith" is the stumbling stone. Some interpret faith to mean praying, working, feeling – and countless other things that have to do with man's efforts and emotions.

Perhaps it is because I, too, used to wonder if I really had "saving faith" that I have so much sympathy and patience with those who do not understand. I grant you it is a miserable position to be in. *It is not God's will that we live in uncertainty*: It is His will that we *know* and understand what "believing" means. Therefore I want to tell you, as simply as I know how, *what it means to believe on the Lord Jesus Christ.*

John 1:12: "But as many as *received Him*, to them *gave He power* to become the sons of God, even to them that *believe on His name.*"

You know that Jesus is the Saviour, and that according to Romans 3:23, ". . . *All have sinned*, and come short of the glory of God." All are born in sin and are therefore on the road to hell. You know that Jesus took your place, He died for you–your substitute, your Saviour. You also know that before His death can help you, you must RECEIVE Him of your own free will. Now, you have acknowledged yourself a sinner and know in your heart that you want to be saved. *You know that by receiving Jesus you can be saved*, but your problem is *HOW to receive Jesus.*

You have never seen Him. If you could reach out now and literally put your hand in His nail-scarred hand, that would be easy–and you would not hesitate to say, "Yes, Jesus, I will take you as my Saviour." But you cannot do that, and some of you do not know how you will know when you *have* received Him. The most simple way I know to show you how to receive Christ by faith and to *know* when you are saved is just this:

Romans 10:13 says, "*For whosoever shall call upon the name of the Lord shall be saved.*" In other words, *God* says, "*I* have given you the record of how *I love you*, and *I* have sent Jesus into the world to die for you. *I* have told you that if you will receive *My Son I* will make you My child. You will not be an adopted child–but *I* will give you a new birth, you will be *born into My family* and become *My child* (John 1:13). *I* have told you all of this in *My Word.* Now when you are ready to receive *My Son*, just call–*and I will do the saving*!"

Born Again by the Word

I Peter 1:23 says, "Being born again, not of corruptible seed (like our first birth), but of incorruptible, *by the Word of God*, which liveth and abideth forever." That is what you want, is it not? You want to be born again. God's Word says we are born again by the Word of God. Keep that in mind now as we turn to Ephesians 2:8. (We will use just four passages – turn to them and mark them in your Bible: John 1:12; Romans 10:13; I Peter 1:23; and Ephesians 2:8.)

Saved by Faith

"For by grace are ye saved through faith; and that not of yourselves: it is the gift of God" (Eph. 2:8). We are saved entirely by grace – nothing added, nothing taken away. Salvation is all of God–God's grace; but we receive it by *faith.* (We cannot see Jesus nor literally take hold of Him.) Faith is *believing.* Believing *what*? Peter says we are born again by the Word, so then–we BELIEVE THE WORD. Our faith is in the Word of God–not in our feelings, our prayers, our life, or anything we can do. *Faith is believing God.* (Notice I did not say "believing IN God," but *believing God.*)

God says, "Whosoever shall call upon the name of the Lord shall be saved." God wants you to believe Him. When you call on Him and ask Him to save you, and deep in your heart you sincerely tell Him you will receive Jesus as your Saviour, God wants you to KNOW you are saved because *He said* He would save you. *That is believing God.* He wants you to trust Him to do exactly what He said He would do – *and He said He would save you if you called on Him.*

Does Salvation Produce Feelings?

If you pray for God to save you and then you say, "I know I am saved *because I feel better,*" you have faith in the wrong thing. Some have faith in a dream, some in a vision, some in feelings, and others in emotions. But by the authority of God's Word I declare that if you are basing your salvation on any of those things, you do not have "saving faith." *Saving faith is BELIEVING GOD, instead of believing your feelings.*

We are born again by the Word of God. If faith is believing–then we must believe the Word. I am just as sure I am saved as I am sure this is the Word of God. Now what does this add up to? You hear the record God gives of His Son–that Jesus died for you, and if you will receive Him as your Saviour, God will "born" you into the heavenly family and you will be His child. When you have heard God's plan for your redemption, you call on God and ask Him to save you. (You believe God and trust Him to save you because He said He would.) *Then –you know you are saved because God said He would save you.*

Have you sincerely asked God to save you? Have you believed God? It does not matter how you FEEL about it – God wants you to believe Him and His Word. Peter says, "The Word liveth and abideth forever." Your feelings will never change nor alter the Word of God. The Word never changes – but your feelings do. *Never put your faith in your feelings–but in the Word of God.*

Now let us go back to John 1:12: "As many as received Him . . . ." You know in your own mind and heart that you want to receive Jesus. You know you told God you would receive Jesus and you know you meant it. Any sane person knows whether he wants to receive Jesus and whether or not he really means it when he asks God to save him. The devil does not make you doubt that part; *what he tries to make you doubt and wonder about is whether or not God kept His Word.*

"God Cannot Lie"

". . . It is impossible for God to lie . . ." (Heb. 6:18).

". . . God . . . cannot lie . . ." (Titus 1:2).

When you, the very best you know how, receive Jesus as your Saviour, that is as far as you can go; *the rest is up to God.* Are you going to believe God?

Faith is believing . . .

"Being born again by the Word of God."

So . . . *I am born again by believing God's Word*!

He said if I would call, He would save me. I have sincerely called, *and I know He saved me because He said He would.*

Those who have sincerely called and still do not know whether or not they are saved simply DO NOT BELIEVE GOD. Yes, they believe there IS a God, they believe Jesus died and rose again, they believe God WILL save them – but they are not willing to believe God does save them NOW, thus taking Him at His Word. They are not willing to believe He saved them because He said He would. They want Him to prove His truth by giving them some emotional experience. They are not willing to believe Him on His Word alone. They insult Him by asking for proof that He told the truth. "He that BELIEVETH NOT God hath made Him a liar" (I John 5:10).

Nine out of ten people wait for a "feeling" before they are willing to believe God. They ask God to save them, then tarry for Him to give them a feeling–and *then* they believe Him. Do you not see how wrong this would be? You would then believe because of "*feelings*"–not because of *God's Word.* Those who are not willing to believe God's Word are calling God a liar. "He that believeth on the Son of God hath the witness in himself: *he that believeth not God hath made Him a liar*; because he believeth not the record that God gave of His Son" (I John 5:10).

The record God gave was that He would save whosoever called upon Him for salvation. Anyone who calls upon God and then says he does not know whether or not he is saved *does not believe God* and has made Him a liar.

Oh, how simple salvation is! God wants you to BELIEVE Him. We are saved by GRACE through FAITH. Faith is *believing. What* do we believe? "*Being born again by the Word.*" *Believe it because God said it.* Do not ask for proof; that is not believing God and proves that you do not take Him at His word.

Some people treat God as though they cannot trust His Word. They want proof (in an unusual feeling, a vision or dream) that He meant what He said, and that He did what He said He would do. *Feelings or no feelings, I know I am saved*, praise God, because *I know* His Word is true, and He said He would save me if I called on Him. *I know* I am saved because God said He would save me! I have God's Word for my salvation – *do you*?

May God help you to believe Him. "For what saith the Scripture? Abraham believed God, and it was counted unto him for righteousness" (Rom. 4:3).

"He that rejecteth me, and receiveth not my words, hath one that judgeth him: THE WORD THAT I HAVE SPOKEN, THE SAME SHALL JUDGE HIM in the last day" (John 12:48).

Spiritual Growth is Different

I believe many people have difficulty in "believing" because they have salvation and Christian growth confused. We have discussed salvation by faith, but Christian growth is an entirely different matter.

I Peter 2:2 says, "As newborn babes, desire the sincere milk of the Word, that ye may grow thereby."

After we are born into God's family by the Word of God, we grow. In this, many become confused. They expect to be and want to be mature Christians when they are just newborn babes. The older we grow in grace, the more we will read the Word. The longer we live for Jesus, the more joy we have. "Every day with Jesus is sweeter than the day before."

Take God at His word; do not doubt Him any longer. *Be saved NOW – and have the assurance of your salvation*!

"And this is the record, that God hath given to us eternal life, and this life is in His Son. He that hath the Son hath life; and he that hath not the Son of God hath not life. These things have I written unto you that believe on the name of the Son of God; that ye may know that ye have eternal life, and that ye may believe on the name of the Son of God" (I John 5:11–13).

THAT SETTLES IT!